PRAISE FOR THE CLOTH EDITION

"The *Washington Post* embedded Juliet Eilperin on Capitol Hill for the embattled first years of the on-going Republican so-called revolution. *Fight Club Politics* is a distillation of her dispatches from the trenches of the House of Representatives, giving many gruesome details about who did what to whom. Readers can learn here why Congressional politics these days is not for sissies, and only occasionally for the minimally civil."

—Nelson W. Polsby, author of *How Congress Evolves*, professor of political science, University of California, Berkeley

"In this lucidly written and thoroughly researched first book, *Washington Post* reporter and D.C. native Eilperin posits that, beginning with Newt Gingrich's nomination as House Speaker in 1994, war-like tactics, manipulation and strategic takeovers have replaced compromise within the House of Representatives, consequently polarizing America's two major parties and leaving the views of its ordinary citizens underrepresented. Eilperin portrays Gingrich as an intimidating, conflicted and sometimes disturbing figure who consolidated Republican power early in his tenure, strong-arming committee chairmen and even soliciting political advice from friend Joe Paterno, the Penn State football coach. To maintain control, the Republican leadership uses loopholes in the system, such as introducing bills so late that representatives don't have time to review them before voting. And the Democrats are shown responding in kind, sticking with their own and ranting bitterly about the Republican House majority. Eilperin's years of experience as a House reporter show in her well-chosen and insightful quotations from lawmakers and commentators, her buoyant prose and the wide scope of her argument. Her portrayal of the fallen House is utterly convincing, but Eilperin ends hopefully, with a look toward what's necessary to restore balance. This exemplary volume is a good bet for anyone wanting an insider's view of America's corridors of power."

—*Publishers Weekly*

"It would be difficult to be more fair and balanced than Eilperin has been. . . . While she finds both Republicans and Democrats at fault for the current state of affairs, her journalistic analysis of the 'dysfunctional' House hold Republicans responsible, in particular, for failing to honor their promises."

—*FindLaw*

"In her years reporting on the House, Eilperin discovered many of [Congress's] dysfunctions, maladies that she describes accurately and admirably."

—*Washington Post Book World*

". . . a skillfully concise treatment of House politics since the early 1990s."

—John J. Pitney Jr., Claremont McKenna College, in *National Review Online*

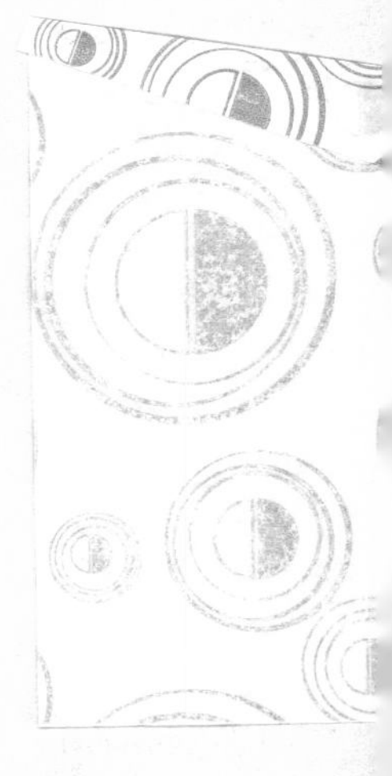

FIGHT CLUB POLITICS

HOOVER STUDIES
IN POLITICS, ECONOMICS,
AND SOCIETY

General Editors
Peter Berkowitz and Tod Lindberg

OTHER TITLES IN THE SERIES

Uncertain Shield:
The U.S. Intelligence System
in the Throes of Reform
by Richard A. Posner

Warrant for Terror:
Fatwas of Radical Islam
and the Duty to Jihad
by Shmuel Bar

Preventing Surprise Attacks:
Intelligence Reform
in the Wake of 9/11
by Richard A. Posner

FIGHT CLUB POLITICS

How Partisanship Is Poisoning the House of Representatives

Juliet Eilperin

HOOVER STUDIES
IN POLITICS, ECONOMICS,
AND SOCIETY

Published in cooperation with
HOOVER INSTITUTION
Stanford University • Stanford, California

ROWMAN & LITTLEFIELD PUBLISHERS, INC.
Lanham • Boulder • New York • Toronto • Oxford

ROWMAN & LITTLEFIELD PUBLISHERS, INC.

The Hoover Institution on War, Revolution and Peace, founded at Stanford University in 1919 by Herbert Hoover, who went on to become the thirty-first president of the United States, is an interdisciplinary research center for advanced study on domestic and international affairs. The views expressed in its publications are entirely those of the authors and do not necessarily reflect the views of the staff, officers, or Board of Overseers of the Hoover Institution.

www.hoover.org

Published in the United States of America
by Rowman & Littlefield Publishers, Inc.
A wholly owned subsidiary of The Rowman & Littlefield Publishing Group, Inc.
4501 Forbes Boulevard, Suite 200, Lanham, Maryland 20706
www.rowmanlittlefield.com
PO Box 317
Oxford
OX2 9RU, UK
Distributed by National Book Network

Copyright © 2006 by the Board of Trustees of the Leland Stanford Junior University
Published in cooperation with the Hoover Institution at Stanford University.
Afterword to paperback edition copyright © 2007 by the Board of Trustees of the
Leland Stanford Junior University
First paperback edition, 2007

All rights reserved. No part of this publication may be reproduced, stored in a retrieval system, or transmitted in any form or by any means, electronic, mechanical, photocopying, recording, or otherwise, without written permission of the publisher.

First printing, 2006; first paperback printing, 2007
13 12 11 10 09 08 07 9 8 7 6 5 4 3 2 1
Manufactured in the United States of America

British Library Cataloguing in Publication Information Available

The hardback edition of this book was previously catalogued by the Library of Congress as follows:

Library of Congress Cataloging-in-Publication Data
Eilperin, Juliet.
Fight club politics : how partisanship is poisoning the House of Representatives / Juliet Eilperin
p. cm. — (Hoover studies in politics, economics, and society)
Includes bibliographical references and index.
ISBN-13: 978-0-7425-5118-3 (cloth : alk. paper)
ISBN-10: 0-7425-5118-0 (cloth : alk. paper)
1. United States—Congress—House. 2. United States—Congress—House—Election districts. 3. Political parties—United States—History. 4. Apportionment (Election law)—United States—History. 5. Election districts—United States.
JK1341.E55 2006
328.73/072—dc22 2006920641

ISBN-10: 0-7425-5119-9 (paper : alk. paper)
ISBN-13: 978-0-7425-5119-0 (paper : alk. paper)

∞™ The paper used in this publication meets the minimum requirements of American National Standard for Information Sciences—Permanence of Paper for Printed Library Materials, ANSI/NISO Z39.48-1992.

To my grandmother
Maria G. Cook,
who stood watch as
I leapt into the water

"Politics is the sport of kings."
—Huey Long

CONTENTS

ACKNOWLEDGMENTS

I'll confess at the outset that I wrote this book mainly in order to write an effusive set of acknowledgments. So with the reader's indulgence, I'll briefly thank some of the people who have given me moral and intellectual support over the past three-and-a-half decades.

Peter Berkowitz first suggested I write this book in November 2004 over an excellent Italian meal one night in Cleveland Park. I am grateful that he and others at the Hoover Institution—Tod Lindberg, John Raisian, David Brady, and Jeff Bliss—and the staff at Rowman & Littlefield thought I had something worthwhile to say after spending a decade covering the House, and that he and Tod served as such skillful editors.

I would never have been able to write this modest volume without my idyllic spring 2005 sabbatical at Princeton University, where I taught political reporting and consumed large amounts of Flavia tea at the Joseph Henry House. The entire staff of the Humanities Council—Carol Rigolot, Michelle French, Lin DeTitta, and Cass Garner—made me feel at home, and Professor Gary Bass served as the best Princeton sherpa a woman could ever desire. I am indebted to my Humanities 441 students, who made me happy each Tuesday afternoon as soon as I walked into the seminar.

For the past eight years I have been lucky enough to work in one of the best newsrooms in America, filled with kind and generous colleagues. Many offered thoughts on this book, including Mike Abramowitz, Peter Baker, Dan Balz, Tom Edsall, and Susan Glasser. Susan gave me my start on Capitol Hill, and I hope I can keep working by her side for the next thirty years or so. *The Washington Post*'s news research team boasts a bevy of dogged investigators, and Carl Evanzz, Madonna Lebling, Don Pohlman, Lucy Shackelford, Meg Smith, and Derek Willis were always willing to track down obscure facts and quotes for me. Maralee Schwartz and Ceci Connolly have always been on my side, and I love them for it. Helen Dewar has served as a role model since I started reading her work in elementary school; Helen, along with David Broder, Dan Morgan, Eric Pianin, and Jim Vandehei helped me probe the inner workings of Congress during my time as the *Post*'s House reporter. Liz Spayd allowed me time to research and write this book, while Shankar Vendatam generously covered for me while I was gone. The rest of the *Post*'s science reporters—David Brown, Guy Gugliotta, Marc Kaufman, Rob Stein, and Rick Weiss—always manage to crack me up on deadline, which I view as an essential component of my work. I have also enjoyed the support of many talented bosses, including Chuck Babington and my current mentor-in-chief, Nils Bruzelius.

I have to thank Sam Hirsch and Nathaniel Persily, two men who are almost as fascinated by backroom politicking and voters' behavior as I am, for sharing their vast legal knowledge with me. Bruce Josten operated as sort of an unofficial research assistant, sending me constant e-mail messages on the latest redistricting developments. David Greenberg served as my title consultant in between reading his son Leo bedtime stories, while Joshua Wolf Shenk added in his two cents in the midst of his own book launch. Mark Allen reminded me that any decent political book must pay homage—at least once—to his great home state of Louisiana. Gloria Dittus and her team taught me the art of public relations, Abby Weintraub gave me artistic advice, and David Weller gave me a sense of what it means to actually sell a book. Equally important, I received invaluable help from the dozens of lawmakers, lobbyists, and political operatives who shared their insights with me on how Washington has changed over the past few decades.

My family—my grandmother Maria G. Cook; my mother, Sophie Cook; my father, Stephen Eilperin; my stepmother, Michelle Hester; my brother, Michael Demos; and my sister-in-law, Ali Demos—have insisted since I was tiny that I could pursue any career I wanted, and I couldn't have entered journalism without their backing. My brother took endless calls from me about this book on his cell phone, while my father edited this manuscript so deftly I'm tempted to make him screen all my future copy. Mark Wiedman—who has offered me sage advice on all things personal and professional for more than a dozen years—served as my other most trusted reader, and I owe him an enormous debt.

Most of all I would like to thank the family I choose: David Plotz and Hanna Rosin, Nina Morrison and Carina Biggs, Dan Mach and Kim Parker, Gillian Weiss and Elliot Posner, Sara Sklaroff and Kevin Carey, and Alice and David DeMallie. My friends' unwavering faith and devotion allowed me to write this book, and it is the reason my life is as rich and as joyful as it is.

Juliet Eilperin
Washington, D.C.

Author's Note: This book was written and published during the 109th Congress, and the titles of lawmakers mentioned during the course of its narrative reflect the positions they occupied during that time.

INTRODUCTION

Revolution and Redistricting

I don't object to polarization if it achieves an objective.
—Former House Speaker
Newt Gingrich (R-Ga.)

I used to love this game, until Newt spoiled it.
—Wisconsin Representative
David Obey, top Democrat on the
House Appropriations Committee

Just after being nominated as House Speaker in December 1994, Newt Gingrich (R-Ga.) instructed newly elected GOP members to read how the Duke of Wellington had defeated the French in the Peninsular War in the early 1800s. In a situation where "the French have overwhelming military superiority and Wellington has to win by strategy because he can't possibly win in a straight-up fight," Gingrich saw several parallels to himself.

A former Army brat, the Republican leader envisioned himself as an ideological warrior using military tactics to prevail in the public arena. At times Gingrich relied on military indoctrination proper: in

Epigraphs. Newt Gingrich, interview with author, Feb. 27, 2005; David Obey, interview with author, Feb. 10, 2005.

1995 he dispatched half a dozen colleagues to learn about war operations at the army's Training and Doctrine Command Center in Fort Monroe, Virginia. The Pentagon picked up the bill.

"On the one front we always knew we would have the Democratic Party, the labor unions, the trial lawyers, and the left-wing activists and most of the media—this was a pre-FOX era," Gingrich recalled, referring to the conservative news channel. "We had to fight a maneuver campaign in which you had to have working control of your team if you were focused on getting things done. . . . We were simultaneously consolidating our grip on the country, setting the stage for the 2000 election, and getting our policy goals while steadily weakening the liberal Democratic wing of America."[1]

Gingrich began waging his own high-stakes Peninsular campaign as soon as he took over the House. He hastened to banish any vestiges of the House's Democratic rule, to establish a new model for governing the body, and to push for the ambitious policies outlined in the GOP's "Contract with America." Gingrich figured he would have at most six years to pursue his revolutionary goals, and he was willing to take drastic action to accomplish them.

In doing so, he remade the House of Representatives. And all Americans, lawmakers and citizens alike, have been living with the consequences from Gingrich's campaign ever since.

The Republicans' victory in 1994 marked the culmination of a protracted battle over the House of Representatives, a prize that Democrats had held for forty years before Gingrich's triumph. The 435-member "people's House" occupies a unique place in the American political system: because of the frequency of its election cycles, its members are meant to be closest to ordinary citizens and to mirror the politics and the prejudices of the U.S. public. The House is a

1. Gingrich interview.

diverse place, relatively speaking: when the GOP took control in 1995, the chamber boasted forty-eight women, thirty-eight African Americans, seventeen Latinos, and seven Asian Americans and Pacific Islanders. While law ranked as the dominant profession in that 104th Congress (as it had for years before), there were fourteen fewer lawyers than the year before. Moreover, the new body boasted four funeral directors, three dentists, two automobile assembly line workers, two veterinarians, a florist, a riverboat captain, a jewelry maker, and a taxi driver.[2]

House members represent smaller groups of voters than their Senate and presidential counterparts—roughly 640,000 people, depending on the state—and face reelection more frequently, every two years. The House, which operates on majority rule and without the same elaborate procedures as the Senate, often drives public debate by passing legislation that goes faster and further than senators or the president might want.

The Capitol where these lawmakers work is a neoclassical behemoth, a cluttered mix of marbled floors and Constantino Brumidi frescoes jumbled together with high-speed wireless access, C-SPAN cameras, and Starbucks coffee outlets. It is a place House Republicans set out to discredit, and destroy, so they could rebuild it in their own image.

At the same time Gingrich and his lieutenants were revamping Congress from the inside, party operatives far away from the Capitol

2. Congressional Research Service Report 95-2000, "Membership of the 104th Congress: A Profile," Jan. 25, 1995, 1–3. However an *Austin American-Statesman* editorial, published shortly after the GOP won control, noted that if the 104th Congress accurately reflected the nation it would have included 222 women, 52 African Americans, 39 Latinos, and 13 Asians. "A Lopsided Congress Needs Honest Views on Affirmative Action," *Austin American-Statesman*, Mar. 26, 1995.

The current 109th Congress is even more diverse than its predecessors: it has a record number of 65 women and 68 racial or ethnic minority members. Susan Milligan, "New Congress Is Most Diverse Ever," *Boston Globe*, Nov. 6, 2004.

were reshaping the country's political landscape through redistricting. The traditional decennial rite in which the country divvies up citizens into voting blocs and maps out new congressional seats in all fifty states is a wonkish one, with a handful of practitioners working largely behind closed doors to determine politicians and constituents' fates. Redistricting may seem impenetrable to outsiders, but it explains how GOP leaders have successfully pursued policies that reflect their own beliefs, as well as those of their adherents, while leaving many other Americans by the wayside.

Anyone who wondered whether redistricting matters in our current political system got a clear answer on September 28, 2005, when a grand jury in Austin, Texas, indicted House Majority Leader Tom DeLay (R-Tex.) of criminally conspiring with two political associates to funnel illegal corporate donations into 2002 state elections. The fund-raising gambit by DeLay and his allies helped their party take over the Texas House for the first time in 130 years, allowing the GOP to redraw Texas' congressional map a year later so it could solidify its once-thin majority in Washington. While DeLay denied the charges, telling reporters, "I have the facts, the law and the truth on my side," he had to step aside as majority leader.[3] The fallout from the unprecedented indictment, coupled with the growing scandal involving GOP lobbyist and DeLay confidant Jack Abramoff, has already tarnished the national GOP and may end the careers of several prominent lawmakers. On Jan. 3, 2006 Abramoff pled guilty in federal court to fraud, tax evasion and conspiracy to bribe public officials; four days later DeLay abandoned his bid to become majority leader again, and he ultimately resigned from the House in June.

The creation of politically safe, more ideologically tilted congressional seats through redistricting over the past two decades, moreover, has produced two major consequences that extend far beyond Texas. It has cemented the Republicans' hold on power and ensured that

3. R. Jeffrey Smith, "DeLay Indicted in Texas Finance Probe: He Steps Aside as House GOP Leader to Fight Conspiracy Charge in State Elections," *Washington Post*, Sept. 29, 2005.

more politicians from both the extreme left and right have Washington sinecures, from which they face little chance of being ousted. This is the story of how the House of Representatives became the House of Unrepresentatives.[4]

House Republicans are not the only ones responsible for this modern predicament. Their Democratic counterparts have balked at legislative compromise and have crafted election-proof districts across the nation as well. Both parties have used hardball tactics that have polarized Washington, with Democrats and Republicans alike punishing members who cross party lines and rewarding loyalists with generous campaign contributions. From House Minority Leader Nancy Pelosi's (D-Calif.) private tongue lashings of Democrats who supported the GOP's 2003 Medicare prescription drug plan to then-House Minority Leader Richard A. Gephardt's (D-Mo.) use of face paint and a kilt to rally his troops as "Braveheart" before the 2000 election, Democrats have been waging a daily war in Washington against the GOP as unrelenting and nearly as virulent as that of their counterparts on the other side of the aisle.

Both sides openly acknowledge that politics in the House has become more about strategy than policy. When asked to describe the House Democrats' overall legislative strategy while in the minority, Pelosi spokesman Brendan Daly responded, "It's not about governing. We're focused on message."[5] Or as Charles N. Kahn III—who worked as a senior GOP House aide for more than a decade before leaving to head the Federation of American Hospitals—put it in an interview in December 2004, "It's become Newt Gingrich versus Newt Gingrich."[6] And in this sort of fight, the strongest tactician carries the day.

4. I owe this phrase in part to Jenner & Block attorney Sam Hirsch, who wrote the law review article "The United States House of Unrepresentatives: What Went Wrong in the Latest Round of Congressional Redistricting," *Election Law Journal* 2, no. 2 (2003).

5. Brendan Daly, interview with author, Mar. 10, 2005. Daly has outlined a different vision of Pelosi's leadership since she won election as House speaker in January 2007.

6. Chip N. Kahn III, interview with author, Dec. 16, 2004.

Demographic changes across the United States have exacerbated the divide between Republicans and Democrats inside the Beltway. Americans are increasingly choosing to live with like-minded neighbors, a kind of political segregation that gives lawmakers on the far left and far right a boost in the election calculus. In addition, fewer House members have opted to move their families to Washington in recent decades, a trend that limits the opportunities for lawmakers to get to know each other. Both these factors have made it more difficult for House members to understand each other and their differing points of view.

Indeed, it is hard to exaggerate how much House Republicans and Democrats dislike each other these days. The much-discussed red state–blue state divide captures the duality, but not the animus, of this relationship. They speak about their opponents as if they hail from a distant land with strange customs, all of which are twisted. Republicans see members of the minority as a bunch of sore losers who assail them on procedural grounds because they lack a compelling vision of how to rule the country. Democrats view the GOP majority as a ruthless band that will do anything to maintain its power. When asked to describe each other in interviews for this book, House members used words like "control freak," "childish," "asinine," and "whiners."

Political observers have written and spoken at length about the symptoms of political polarization: the two parties' scorched-earth approach to judicial nominations, the partisan drive to impeach Bill Clinton, and the Democrats' scorn toward President Bush. And the idea of a modern "culture war" has captured the media's attention, as reporters chronicle communities that provide a study in contrasts, with gun-toting religious conservatives on one side and Chardonnay-sipping atheist lefties on another. The irony is that while many U.S. voters are more complex than these stereotypes, sometimes their elected representatives are not.

But fewer analysts have looked at the problem's roots: how some of our nation's highest-ranking officials have fostered a divide through redistricting and internal congressional reforms that will last for years to come, regardless of popular sentiment. House members—aided by their state counterparts—have rigged the system to guarantee that they, and politicians who think like them, return to Washington year after year. And once they arrive, House leaders on both sides go to extraordinary lengths to reinforce the partisan divide, worsening an already tense situation.

Over the past decade Republicans have succeeded in realizing their original reformist vision of the House, making the chamber more efficient, less burdened by patronage, and more responsive to a specific constituency: conservative Republicans. Their quest to consolidate power, however, has overwhelmed their earlier genuine attempts to reform Congress. They have undermined the institution's attentiveness to public sentiment by silencing GOP moderates and the more than two hundred Democrats who have won the right to represent millions of Americans.

This is not to say that House Democrats ruled the chamber fairly before they lost the majority: they pioneered many of the repressive tactics now favored by GOP leaders. But part of Republican revolutionaries' allure lay in how they vowed to reclaim the House for the American public, and they should be judged by that standard.

In one sense the House is now a better-oiled machine than it used to be. Republican leaders routinely pass legislation on an array of topics, from curbing class action suits to revamping the United Nations. But on a more profound level, the chamber is dysfunctional. Democratic leaders are tangential to governing, devoting most of their time to issuing press releases, complaining of their ill treatment, and drafting policies that have no chance of making it into law. A few conservative rank-and-file Democrats have the opportunity to shape legislation, but their influence is limited and they must endure constant taunts from their more liberal colleagues. Moderate Republicans experience the same sort of hectoring when they attempt to forge common ground with the minority. In this highly contentious environment, bipartisan cooperation amounts to betrayal.

Now members from both parties are worried that their leaders are losing touch with the citizenry. New Hampshire Representative Charlie Bass, a moderate and a member of the Class of 1994 that helped deliver the majority to the GOP, fears that House Speaker J. Dennis Hastert (R-Ill.) and DeLay are today as deaf to popular opinion as the Democratic barons they felled a decade before. While today's Republicans may not be any more despotic than the heavy-handed Democratic chairmen of the 1970s and 1980s, they have failed to live up to their own promises of reform.

"The leadership ought to be prepared to lose from time to time," Bass said. "The opposition just doesn't exist. I think the public would become enthusiastic about issues in Congress if there was some surprise about how it would come out."[7]

As a reporter covering the House from 1994 to 2004—first for the *States News Service* and for *Roll Call* newspaper before joining *The Washington Post* in 1998—I saw firsthand how Republican revolutionaries worked to solidify their control and dismantle institutions that promoted compromise, even as they took steps to reform Congress. And I witnessed how Democrats responded in kind, becoming more partisan and wedded to interest groups that drove the two parties further apart.

A variety of factors—including more sophisticated political mapping techniques, House rules that have curtailed dissent, and more powerful party leaders—have fostered this national divide. Lawmakers have become less accountable to the public and more beholden to the party apparatus, which in turn has encouraged them to become more ideologically entrenched and less inclined to reflect voters' broad political interests and views. This book will show how we have come to a point where average Americans have little say over what happens in the House, and what can be done about it.

7. Charlie Bass, interview with author, Nov. 23, 2004.

CHAPTER 1

Revamping the House of Representatives

> We were on a hell of a strut, weren't we? We strutted around.
>
> —Former House Majority Leader Richard K. Armey (R-Tex.)

After enjoying decades of unrivaled control, Democrats became increasingly dictatorial in the 1980s. The chamber's leaders—nervous about the prospect of losing power—adopted a more confrontational attitude toward the GOP minority with whom they had worked in the past. First House Speaker Thomas P. "Tip" O'Neill (D-Mass.), and then his successor Jim Wright (D-Tex.), started cracking down on House Republicans even when it did not make the difference between winning or losing a vote. They limited opportunities for debate, publicly mocked members of the minority, and frequently denied Republicans the chance to make their mark on legislation.

Part of this adversarial jousting stemmed from a genuine ideolog-

Epigraph. Richard K. Armey, interview with author, Jan. 27, 2005.

ical difference between the liberal House leadership and conservative Republicans, who had found an influential ally in President Reagan. These two camps had different views of how government should operate, and they fought bitter battles over everything from supporting the Nicaraguan contra rebels to funding America's arms buildup. With more at stake in terms of policy, the fight between the two parties intensified.

From the 1950s to the 1970s, the two parties feuded often, but they shared a more similar position on taxes, spending, regulation, and use of armed force than today's Republicans and Democrats do. The parties were less ideologically based: a broad swath of the GOP accepted the welfare state, while many Democrats backed the military. The current congressional fight reflects a much larger policy conflict (as well as a blatant power grab by influential leaders and a skewed political map).

House Democratic leaders' heavy-handed tactics made headlines and infuriated even some of the most moderate GOP members. Wright managed to get through a 1987 budget bill, for example, by adjourning the House and then calling it back into session twenty minutes later on the grounds that it constituted a "new" legislative day. In a 1987 election dispute over what became known as the "Bloody Eighth," Democrats insisted on seating Democrat Frank McCloskey as the House member from Indiana's Eighth District although state officials had declared his GOP opponent, Richard McIntyre, the winner. O'Neill dressed down Gingrich on the House floor after the combative Republican delivered a fiery late-night speech, a highly unorthodox move, and refused a customary straight vote on President Reagan's 1981 budget. Instead he split it into seven parts.

Most of these efforts backfired: in the case of Reagan's 1981 budget, the House passed it anyway with the backing of conservative Democrats. And when Democrats prevailed legislatively, as in the Bloody Eighth, they lost politically by strengthening the hand of Gingrich and other activists, who could convincingly argue to rank-and-file Republicans that the GOP would get nowhere by playing by the rules.

Instead Gingrich, Richard K. Armey (R-Tex.), and other backbenchers embarked on an unprecedented campaign of their own to convince Americans that they needed to overthrow the established order. This cadre of younger Reaganites was not willing to accommodate senior Democrats and embraced the daunting task of winning back the majority. They launched a sustained attack, questioning House leaders' ethics, and focused on crafting an alternative policy agenda rather than on pursuing legislative compromises with the majority.

Several Democratic leaders, who treated the House as their personal fiefdom, gave these Republicans ample fodder. Jim Wright entered into a book deal that tapped into a host of eager buyers from the D.C. lobbying community, selling a collection of largely repackaged speeches to interest groups in bulk—for which he received a 55 percent royalty share—in order to circumvent the speaking fee limit that lawmakers faced at the time. (Now members of Congress cannot accept any honoraria at all.) This arrangement touched off an ethics probe that led to his 1989 resignation after investigators concluded he had taken unfair advantage of his post to peddle his book. In what became known as the House bank scandal, investigators discovered that a slew of members had routinely run financial overdrafts without facing any consequences. The ensuing hoopla—the offenders' names became public—tarnished the chamber's reputation even further. House members' government accounts had essentially become a free revolving loan fund, a privilege ordinary Americans did not enjoy.

Republicans tapped into voters' unease by portraying the House as an evil institution: Representative Jim Nussle (R-Ia.) demonstrated his outrage on national television by appearing on the House floor with a paper bag over his head, declaring he was ashamed to be a member of the House. Shortly before the Republican takeover, Gingrich's political action committee, GOPAC, came up with a series of "contrast words" Republican candidates could use against their opponents. The phrase list included "decay, failure, shallow, traitors, pathetic, corrupt, incompetent, sick."[1]

Some moments of conciliation still emerged in the waning days of the House Democratic majority, such as the 1990 budget deal in which President George H. W. Bush agreed to reverse his "read my lips" pledge and to raise taxes as part of a larger accord with congressional Democrats. And Robert H. Michel (R-Ill.), as House minority leader, continued to seek compromises with the majority.

But Gingrich showed little interest in these agreements. During the 1990 budget negotiations he spent most of his time flipping through magazines, prompting then-House Majority Leader Richard Gephardt to complain to White House officials.[2] Privately, many Republicans stewed over how Democrats treated them. House Energy and Commerce Committee Chairman John D. Dingell (D-Mich.) kept 82 percent of his panel's staff and 77 percent of its budget for his side while giving the remains to the minority, which enraged Republicans like Gingrich.[3] Dingell defends this allocation today, saying, "I gave them every damn thing they asked for. . . . We just left the Republicans to do their business. Did I give them one-third of the staff? No, I didn't. I didn't see why I had to."[4]

The future Speaker and his allies devoted much of their time to plotting behind the scenes on how to overthrow the establishment, and the Democrats' dismissive treatment of minority members merely fueled their sense of purpose. On one occasion, Gingrich huddled in

1. Martin Walker, "Republicans' Fiery Avenger; Newt Gingrich Takes Up His Powerful New Washington Role Determined to Dismantle the U.S. Welfare State," *Guardian* (London), Dec. 5, 1994.

2. Richard A. Gephardt, interview with author, June 16, 2005.

3. House Administration Committee records.

4. John D. Dingell, interview with author, June 28, 2005.

a room with allies like Walker, Vin Weber (R-Minn.), and Connie Mack (R-Fla.), and the men grumbled about how the majority expected them to take "the crumbs off the floor" that the Democrats pushed from the table.[5] Once Republicans gained power, they had little interest in treating Democrats gently.

Some junior Republicans became so enamored of negative attacks they stopped worrying about whether the attacks were rooted in actual substance. In one typical Capitol Hill scene in 1993, Senator Robert Dole (R-Kans.) sauntered by a group of young House Republicans standing in line to tape satellite feeds, sponsored by the National Republican Congressional Committee, all of which entailed bashing President Clinton.

"Hello gentlemen! What are we against today?" Dole asked, as he made his way over to confer with Bob Michel.

"We don't know yet sir, but we're going to make damn sure it doesn't happen!" one House Republican lawmaker replied.[6]

Breaking with the past, these Republican rebels didn't want to adhere to the traditional way of doing business in Washington. Armey, who served as House majority leader for four terms before retiring in 2003, looked with scorn on compliant House Republicans who cozied up to Democratic committee chairs the way academics are constantly "trying to please their old thesis advisers. They were so conditioned to making that guy happy."[7]

Armey couldn't have cared less about making men like Dingell, or other senior Democrats, happy.

After shocking the Democrats, many political pundits, and even Republicans by winning control of the House in 1994, GOP revolu-

5. Former House GOP staffers present at the meeting who asked not to be identified, interview with author, Mar. 23, 2005.

6. Scot Montrey, e-mail exchange with author, Feb. 28, 2005.

7. Armey interview.

tionaries enacted a series of brash changes aimed at making the chamber more accountable to the public. They had appealed to the public by vowing both to consider popular legislative initiatives that had been stymied in the past—such as the balanced budget amendment and term limits on lawmakers—and to make the House more accountable to the public. While several legislative planks of the GOP's "Contract with America" didn't make it into law in the end, Republicans enjoyed considerable success in changing the way the House did business.

When Newt Gingrich unveiled the party's Contract with America on the Capitol steps on September 27, 1994, he promised, "If the American people accept this contract, we will have begun the journey to renew American civilization."[8] Less than two weeks later, he pledged to make the chamber into "a more humane House."[9] Nussle, who had gained national prominence by wearing a paper bag over his head, oversaw the transition to House Republican rule and said shortly after assuming his post, "Everything is open for review, and change will be considered for every single issue. There will be a new order."[10]

Republicans started their first day in power by applying several federal laws to the House and Senate—something that had never been done before—through the Congressional Accountability Act. This allowed the Capitol's blue-collar workforce to unionize for the first time and to pursue work-related discrimination claims in the same way other federal workers had for years. House leaders launched the THOMAS website so that ordinary citizens could track legislation in real time. (Citizens can now even send their testimony by e-mail

8. David E. Rosenbaum, "Republicans Offer Voters a Deal for Takeover of the House," *New York Times*, Sept. 28, 1994.

9. Richard Wolff, "Newt's World: Leader Plans 'to Transform' Government," *USA Today*, Nov. 16, 1994.

10. Richard Whittle, "Republicans Vow More Humane House: Leaders Pledge to Make Time for Families, Not to Take Revenge on Democrats," *Dallas Morning News*, Nov. 15, 1994.

to committees.) The leadership sought to regularize the House's finances by tasking an independent accounting firm to conduct an internal House audit. The accountants determined that the chamber's record keeping was so shoddy it was impossible to draw any solid conclusions about the House's finances. In fact, it took until their fourth audit in 1998 for the House to receive a clean bill of health.

The House's new leaders also professionalized the chamber's staff, abolishing patronage havens like the House mailroom and installing managers who modeled the Capitol on the corporate world. And they banned all gifts to lawmakers and staff from outside groups, though they modified the measure after members complained that it was cutting them off from their constituents.

Several of these changes saved money: the House Oversight Committee estimated it cut costs by $50 million in 1995 by eliminating 621 committee staff positions and by halting the daily delivery of ice to House offices, among other reforms. House Republicans bolstered the Office of the Inspector General by increasing its staff to twenty and by giving it a $4 million budget. Under new rules lawmakers could not make free use of the House recording studio as an election neared, unless the race was uncontested or the member's name did not appear on the ballot.[11]

The House GOP adopted other institutional changes aimed at dismantling the Democrats' way of governance. Gingrich and his cohorts abolished proxy voting, compelling lawmakers to stay at lengthy markups if they wanted their votes to count. And House Republicans imposed term limits not just on committee chairs but on the Speaker himself, so as to avoid an ossified leadership in the years to come. (The GOP Conference later reversed itself, so Hastert can serve as Speaker as long as he wants if Republicans keep winning the majority and reelecting him to the post.) They also gave the minority roughly one-third of committee resources compared with the

11. House Administration Committee records.

four- or five-to-one ratio that the Democrats enjoyed while in power. And they guaranteed that on each bill the minority could call for a procedural vote on a "motion to recommit," which allowed Democrats to sketch out an alternative legislative proposal.

Gingrich also set out to transform the relationship between committee chairs and House leaders, a move aimed more at centralizing power than at cleaning up the House. For years liberal Democratic leaders had struggled with how to pursue their goals in an institution largely controlled by autonomous committee chairmen. On some occasions, former House Speaker Tom Foley (D-Wash.) couldn't even entice House Banking Committee Chairman Henry Gonzalez (D-Tex.) into meeting with him, while Wright struggled in vain to convince William Natcher (D-Ky.) on Appropriations to provide increased spending on education for one year.[12] Gingrich made it clear from the outset that committee chairs answered to the leadership and, by extension, to the entire Republican Conference.

"Prior to us power was centered in the chairmen and you had a relatively permissive leadership on the Democratic side that could only maneuver to the degree the chairmen would tolerate," Gingrich recalled. "We had exactly the opposite model: a very strong leadership that operated as a single team—a single team that had lots of tension inside obviously—but nonetheless operated as a single team. And then you had the chairmen who operated within the framework of that leadership."[13]

Gingrich ignored the tradition of seniority and, skipping over several veteran members, installed an old friend from Tulane University, Robert Livingston (R-La.), as chairman of the coveted House Appropriations Committee.

12. House Democratic aides who asked not to be identified, interview with author, Mar. 3, 2005.

13. Gingrich interview.

At times Gingrich struggled to break with tradition. One of his hardest decisions was to pass over Representative Carlos Moorhead (R-Calif.) as head of the Judiciary Committee in favor of Henry J. Hyde (R-Ill.). Moorhead had served the party loyally for years and never caused trouble, but Gingrich viewed Hyde as a more dynamic leader. Torn over what to do, Gingrich called legendary Penn State football coach Joe Paterno, with whom he had struck up a friendship. He asked Paterno whether it was all right to relegate Moorhead to second-tier status despite his lengthy tenure. Paterno likened it to skipping over the senior in line to be quarterback in favor of a younger, more talented player, telling Gingrich that the rest of the House Republican Conference looked to him to make such difficult calls.

"They are depending on you making tough decisions so you can put the best team on the field," Paterno told him. "That is why you are there."[14]

But once he had appointed his lieutenants, Gingrich did not shy away from asserting his authority over committee chairs. When House Transportation and Infrastructure Committee Chairman Bud Shuster (R-Penn.) wanted to exceed budget guidelines as part of a huge public works bill, Gingrich called the panel's entire GOP membership into his office and declared, "We have to go to the [Republican] conference and decide whether Bud's the speaker or I'm speaker."[15] Shuster and his committee members caved.

Another time House Energy and Commerce Committee Chairman Thomas Bliley (R-Va.) had forged a compromise on tobacco with Representative Henry Waxman (D-Calif.) that would have imposed federal regulation, provided a bailout for tobacco farmers, and assessed penalties on tobacco companies who didn't do enough to curb underage smoking. It was an odd marriage between a conser-

14. Dan Meyer, interview with author, Mar. 11, 2005.
15. Gingrich interview.

vative from tobacco country and a liberal who had once publicly humiliated tobacco executives in a nationally televised hearing. Sensing Gingrich's resistance, Waxman made a special plea to the Speaker during a trip to celebrate the fiftieth anniversary of Israel's founding.

"He said, 'That sounds interesting, that sounds reasonable,'" Waxman recalled. "Then he told Bliley, 'Don't you dare bring it up.'"[16]

The committee never considered the bill. As Gingrich explained it in an August 2005 interview, "We didn't think it was to our advantage."[17]

When Republicans first took over, they were a novice majority trying to establish their authority in a narrowly divided House, and their harsh governing tactics during this stage have to be seen in this context. While the House GOP managed to stage a stunning upset in 1994—the Democrats lost fifty-four seats that year while every incumbent Republican won reelection—only twenty-seven seats divided the parties when Gingrich became Speaker, meaning a switch of fourteen votes could translate into a Republican defeat. By contrast, the Democrats had an eighty-one-seat advantage over the Republicans during the 103rd Congress.

Former Representative Robert Walker (R-Penn.), Gingrich's best friend and a procedural expert who helped police the Democrats when the Republicans were in the minority, said he and his colleagues "were naïve at the beginning of the revolution. . . . We had no perception of how hard it is to win every day. All we had to do in the minority is fight a series of glorious fights."[18]

The push to pass all ten planks of the Contract with America, moreover, taught the GOP what Walker now calls "some bad habits," mainly the strategy of adopting legislation on a strict party-line vote.

16. Henry Waxman, interview with author, July 28, 2005.
17. Gingrich interview.
18. Robert Walker, interview with author, Dec. 17, 2004.

"We believed the way you win votes is you hold all of your own party together, rather than reaching out for consensus," Walker said.[19] A handful of bills inspired Democratic support, like the Congressional Accountability Act and a measure aimed at curbing unfunded federal mandates. But the rest of the GOP's initial agenda left most Democrats on the sidelines.

From the outset, House GOP leaders made it clear they would wield their newfound power with a heavy hand. They established committee ratios giving Republicans about two-thirds of the seats, even though the House GOP garnered only 52.4 percent of the vote in 1994.[20] This allowed them to put first-term Republicans like Zach Wamp (Tennessee) and Jon Christensen (Nebraska) on the prized Appropriations and Ways and Means Committees, while Democrats had to ease some of their members off coveted panels. Dingell was forced to lay off dozens of aides after losing his overwhelming staff advantage on the Energy and Commerce Committee, the inevitable cost of losing power.

Even Gingrich acknowledges this dramatic reversal of fortunes damaged his ability to work with newly installed House Minority Leader Richard Gephardt. "Here he is, he's replaced Foley, and he can't deliver anything," Gingrich said. "It was a very painful period, and I don't think our relationship ever recovered from it."[21]

House Republicans also changed the way incoming members learned about Congress. For years new members had attended a bipartisan orientation at Harvard University, as well as joint sessions in Washington. Gingrich sent the Class of 1994 to the conservative Heritage Foundation instead, and held a separate "Speaker's dinner" for his ground troops. For a few years in the late 1990s, members of

19. Walker interview.

20. The House Democrats gave Republicans an even smaller share of the pie when they ruled the chamber, giving the GOP at times a fourth or a fifth of the seats on a given committee.

21. Gingrich interview.

the two parties spent a weekend in Hershey, Pennsylvania, in a retreat aimed at fostering greater civility on Capitol Hill. While the retreat at first attracted two hundred members in 1997, organizers had to abandon it a few years later owing to a lack of interest. Some lawmakers made an effort to revive it for the 109th Congress, but subsequently canceled the program after the November 2004 election.

"The message is loud and clear for freshmen," said Representative Sherrod Brown (D-Ohio). "We'll do it on our own."[22]

Gingrich had set out to create a more modern, ideological, and centrally controlled House, and he succeeded.

In the mid-1990s House revolutionaries also pioneered another aspect of governing: fund-raising. Top congressional leaders doled out money to junior members for years, but Republicans took this to a new level with leadership political action committees (PACs). These campaign coffers, which have proliferated on Capitol Hill over the past two decades, allow lawmakers to attract larger donations than they could accept for their own campaigns, provided they in turn donate the money to other federal candidates. Any House member can accept up to $5,000 each calendar year from a given donor, for example, and then dole it out to other aspiring lawmakers in $5,000 increments per election. Ambitious Republicans saw leadership committees as the best way to unseat House Democrats, by steering campaign contributions to challengers and to junior lawmakers who could not independently attract the big donors' largesse.

Armey was the earliest practitioner of this approach. In 1986 the former economics professor gave $75,000 to House GOP candidates, making him the second most generous incumbent next to Bob Michel. Other Republicans followed suit: when Armey told his colleagues at the leadership table in 1994, "I'm going to pledge half a million dollars, and I'm sure Tom [DeLay] will want to match me," Gingrich was quick to one-up them all, vowing to steer $1 million to

22. Sherrod Brown, interview with author, Feb. 9, 2005.

House GOP candidates.[23] Gingrich saw their "unending campaigning" as essential to maintaining the united backing of his conference, and this approach was important to DeLay's upset victory over Walker in the 1994 majority whip's race. DeLay had raised hundreds of thousands of dollars and traveled to countless districts for many members of the Class of 1994, while Walker had focused more on inside-the-Beltway tactics and policymaking. To this day Walker dislikes leadership PACs, saying they "make leadership elections less competitive on issues of leadership. . . . This leadership PAC thing has gotten out of bounds."[24]

But leadership PACs strengthened the Republican majority on several fronts. They enhanced leaders' standing among rank-and-file members who were grateful for the financial support they couldn't have commanded on their own. The committees made the most efficient use of the GOP's ties to business and other wealthy interests by directing money to key races. And it spurred competition among ambitious members, pouring funds into GOP campaign coffers that might otherwise have gone untapped.

New York Republican Bill Paxon, who chaired the National Republican Congressional Committee during the GOP's victorious 1994 campaign, attributed the party's shift in fund-raising tactics to an empty war chest rather than to a grand strategic vision.

"We did it because we were desperate," Paxon said. "We didn't have any money."[25]

DeLay took this fund-raising approach to a new level in 1999, in an effort to defend Republicans who had backed the impeachment of President Clinton. After analyzing the previous election, the whip and his aides decided they would be best off raising a substantial amount of money early on for these lawmakers, to intimidate potential Democratic challengers. Dubbing the venture Retain Our Majority

23. Armey interview.
24. Walker interview.
25. Bill Paxon, interview with author, Mar. 30, 2005.

Program, or ROMP, DeLay convinced both his whip team and outside lobbyists to muster more than $1.3 million for ten House Republicans, two of whom prosecuted President Clinton and eight of whom voted to impeach him. At the time, DeLay spokesman Michael Scanlon described this unusual way of soliciting lobbyists as a simple matter of efficiency: "There's nothing new going on here. All of the representatives of the business community have a stake in reelecting a Republican majority and we are just expediting that process for them."[26]

ROMP was a success. DeLay held a celebratory lunch at the Capitol Hill Club in June 1999 for the ten targeted Republicans and their lobbyist backers, complete with an oversized check for $1.3 million that was displayed on cue by two of his female staffers. The lobbyist crowd even sounded out a version of a drum roll just before DeLay announced the program's grand fund-raising total.[27] And while two of the program's high-profile beneficiaries lost, the rest won reelection.

As one prominent GOP lobbyist who asked not to be identified observed, "ROMP sent a signal to the downtown [lobbying community] rank-and-file that you are accountable to the leadership for what you do in swing districts. It matters to Tom DeLay what you do in a swing district."[28]

Not to be outdone, Armey headed up a later round of ROMP, summoning several lobbyists to a meeting at the National Republican Congressional Committee to dole out fund-raising assignments. As his aides handed out a list of vulnerable House Republicans, Armey told his downtown allies they should call their clients and instruct them to give money to the ten incumbents. As one participant in the

26. Jim VandeHei, "DeLay Banking on Lobbyists: Private Meeting Sets Cash Goals for Aiding 10 Members," *Roll Call*, May 10, 1999.

27. Juliet Eilperin, "House Whip Wields Fund-Raising Clout; Network of Lobbyists Helps DeLay Gather Millions for GOP Campaigns," *The Washington Post*, Oct. 18, 1999.

28. GOP lobbyist who asked not to be identified, interview with author, Jan. 20, 2005.

meeting put it, "You have the majority leader walking across the street to tell a group of lobbyists, 'This is important to me.' When I call my clients for [Kentucky Republican] Anne Northup, I can now say I'm helping Armey hit his ROMP numbers. It's a totally different thing."[29]

Democratic leaders began copying Republicans' use of leadership PACs to gain influence over junior lawmakers and to solidify their party's financial footing. A month after the Republicans won the majority, Gephardt and his wife Jane had Gingrich and his then-wife, Marianne, over for dinner at Gephardt's Herndon, Virginia, home. (While the exact menu now eludes Gephardt, he thinks they ate chicken. "We're politicians, we go through chicken withdrawal," he explained.)[30]

Gephardt congratulated his Republican counterpart and asked how he had achieved such a stunning victory.

"Money," Gingrich replied.[31]

Gephardt took the lesson seriously, embarking on a frenetic fund-raising drive that amassed millions for his party from the high-tech, as well as the television, movie, and music, industries. In 1999, the latter three industries alone gave House Democrats nearly $1 million, twice what they had given them in 1997 and 1998 combined.[32] Gingrich doled out tens of thousands of dollars from his own campaign war chest to his colleagues, and his successors imitated him. In the run-up to the 2000 election, Nancy Pelosi and Steny Hoyer (D-Md.)—who were vying for the post of minority whip at the time—raised enormous sums for Democratic candidates. Hoyer raised about $1.5 million while Pelosi collected $3.9 million.[33] Now Pelosi and

29. Ibid.

30. Gephardt interview.

31. Ibid.

32. Juliet Eilperin, "And the Winner Is . . . House Democrats; Spacey Heads a Cast of Fundraisers," *The Washington Post*, Mar. 25, 2000.

33. Juliet Eilperin, "The Making of Madam Whip; Fear and Loathing—and Horse Trading—in the Race for the House's No. 2 Democrat," *The Washington Post Magazine*, Jan. 6, 2002.

Hoyer sit atop the House Democrats' leadership ladder, the party's number one and number two, respectively.

ROMP and its Democratic counterpart, Frontline, have now become institutions, a way of rewarding loyal lawmakers and of shunning others. When GOP leaders unveiled their ROMP list for 2005 they left out Representative Christopher Shays, an outspoken Connecticut moderate who barely won reelection the year before. The Democrats publish their own Frontline roster, listing the lucky marginal members who have won the attention of party leaders.

Democrats are just as demanding as Republicans are when it comes to asking their senior members to pony up campaign cash. In late June 2005 Pelosi and her top lieutenants informed their colleagues that if they did not pay their designated "dues for the 2006 election cycle" to the Democratic Congressional Campaign Committee, they could no longer use the phones and other amenities at the DCCC's members services center.

Writing in bold ink and underlining it for emphasis, the June 29 memo warned, "*This policy will be strictly enforced!* We hope that we will not have to deny service to any Member and strongly encourage you to pay your dues so that you can continue taking advantage of our services. The 2006 election is going to be tough and we need *all* of our members to play an active role in our effort to regain the majority."[34]

The leadership PAC frenzy has boosted both the lawmakers' campaign coffers and House leaders' sway over junior members, who are hesitant to anger their political patrons. Party bosses no longer determine which candidate can run for office in a district, but senior House leaders on either side of the aisle can decide whether a given lobbyist cuts a check for a little-known member, or whether these same lobbyists troop to a swing district just before an election to drive voter turnout.

34. Memo to the House Democratic Caucus from the Democratic Leadership, June 29, 2005.

Just before the 2004 election, two ambitious, relatively young Republicans—Eric Cantor (Virginia) and Mike Rogers (Michigan)—sent out competing e-mail messages to lobbyists, inviting them to take part in bus trips from Washington to get out the GOP vote in competitive Pennsylvania House districts. The message to both lobbyists and aspiring House Republicans was clear: these men can deliver for you come election time if they choose to do so. It's the sort of lesson lawmakers remember when they're debating whether to break party ranks, or whom to support in a close leadership election.

Until the late 1990s, companies and unions could give unlimited "soft money" donations to the national parties and party committees, donations that the parties in turn distributed to candidates; now this practice is illegal. As a result wealthy donors have sought other avenues of influence, including leadership PACs. One GOP lobbyist close to the leadership described the burgeoning leadership PAC system as the most effective way of getting campaign contributions to lawmakers in the absence of large "soft money" donations to the party committees.

As Paxon put it, "We've found [that] all the tools to help elect and grow the majority also resulted in electing people who were much more part of the team. It built a pervasive, all-encompassing feeling of loyalty."[35]

Thomas M. Davis III (R-Va.), who chairs the House Government Reform Committee, said the institution of leadership PACs "puts leaders in a stronger position" when they have to extract votes from rank-and-file members on important bills. "Money talks, and big money talks bigger," Davis said.[36]

The current House leaders, Hastert and DeLay, are just as willing as their predecessors to punish recalcitrant lawmakers and to reward

35. Paxon interview.

36. Thomas M. Davis III, interview with author, Feb. 10, 2005.

members of the team. They've made it clear to both current and aspiring committee chairs that bucking the party, either on policy matters or by failing to raise funds aggressively enough, may cost them their jobs.

The 2005 battle to head the House Appropriations Committee exemplified the GOP's prize system: top GOP leaders made it known to the three contenders—Jerry Lewis (R-Calif.), Ralph Regula (R-Ohio), and Hal Rogers (R-Ky.)—that they would have to demonstrate their party loyalty by (a) raising as much money as possible in the 2004 election cycle and (b) pledging to dismiss James W. Dyer, the veteran GOP staff director whom conservatives disliked. All three complied—Rogers raised $1.5 million by the year's end, and Lewis boasted he had raised a total of $25 million over his twenty-five-year congressional tenure. Even Regula, a relative moderate, showed his partisan fervor in 2004 by threatening to eliminate all the projects for Democrats on his subcommittee if they didn't vote for the final bill that year.

In the end Lewis—who enlisted the volunteer aid of lobbyists Ed Buckham, Susan Hirschmann, and Dan Mattoon (all of whom have close ties to Hastert and DeLay)—won the chairmanship. Shortly after assuming the post, Lewis instructed each Appropriations subcommittee chair to establish a leadership political action committee so that they could leverage their positions of power to help more junior Republicans.[37]

But the leadership has little patience for Republicans who get in their way, even if they've got years of seniority. House GOP leaders demoted two of their chairs from the 108th Congress, Ethics Committee Chairman Joel Hefley (R-Colo.) and Veterans Affairs Committee Chairman Christopher Smith (R-N.J.), a move that instilled fear in some ambitious Republicans.

37. GOP lobbyist who asked not to be identified, interview with author, Mar. 11, 2005.

The two men had displeased Hastert and DeLay for different reasons: Smith, who noted that he shepherded thirteen bills into law under his chairmanship, said GOP leaders did not like the fact he authorized generous veterans benefits. "There is a sense of trying to bring people into conformity," he said.[38] Hefley had led a panel that admonished the majority whip twice just before the 2004 elections for conduct unbecoming to the House. Party leaders ousted both men, replacing them with loyalists. (And when two Ethics Committee Republicans questioned the wisdom of removing Hefley, the leadership booted them too.)

A Western iconoclast who likes to ride in rodeos in his spare time as well as paint and sculpt, Hefley was happy to relinquish a post that requires countless hours of hard work and is more of a political liability than an asset. "I'm tickled pink not to have that job," he said after his ouster. But he added in the same interview that he fears the precedent it sets.

"Hastert has a basic sense of fair play and DeLay, I think, is driven by power," Hefley said. The leadership's willingness to penalize its own ethics cops and revamp the rules so that a deadlock on the committee would stave off a formal inquiry rather than trigger it, Hefley added, looks "very much like the arrogance of the Democrats" Republicans toppled in 1994.[39]

Some more centrist Republicans are choosing not to run for the top elected leadership posts, knowing they would have to shift their voting patterns to stay in power. One senior Republican brushed aside a question about running for Speaker or majority leader by saying, "It would put me so out of sync with my district to sit in [leadership] and vote for some of these things, I'd lose my independence."[40]

38. Christopher Smith, interview with author, Feb. 10, 2005.

39. Joel Hefley, interview with author, Feb. 10, 2005. (Hastert reversed course in the spring of 2005 and enacted more bipartisan ethics procedures but kept party loyalists in place on the panel.)

40. Senior House Republican who asked not to be identified, interview with author, Oct. 21, 2005.

House Republicans follow their leaders' guidance for a number of reasons: they tend to be more homogenous as a group than their Democratic counterparts, and their decision to operate as a cohesive unit helped them gain the majority after spending decades in the political wilderness. At the same time, however, some of their unity stems from the fact that rank-and-file members pay a heavy price for challenging their leaders.

"There are rewards for toeing the party line, we all know that, and there are things party leaders can do to you if you don't," said Representative Ray LaHood (R-Ill.), who served as Bob Michel's chief of staff before succeeding his boss in Congress.[41]

While they came to power as rebels, Republicans have imposed the same tight grip on the House that Democrats insisted on in the late 1980s. After a decade in power, they have in some ways morphed into their predecessors. A centralized power structure, coupled with a prolonged and well-cosseted incumbency, has undermined their initial commitment to a more open chamber.

Former Representative Mickey Edwards (R-Okla.), who was the fourth-ranking Republican under Michel's leadership, blames both parties for the current polarization in Congress. "Democrats started this with Jim Wright," Edwards said. "Republicans pledged to be different and they're not. They were for a little while, but they're not now."[42]

41. Ray LaHood, interview with author, Nov. 17, 2004.
42. Mickey Edwards, interview with author, Mar. 8, 2005.

CHAPTER 2

Tearing Washington's Social Fabric Apart

> It's harder than hell to kick somebody on a personal basis when you think you're going to see their wife and kids later in the week. Today that's all gone.
>
> —Representative David Obey (D-Wis.)

> This belief that somehow life today in the United States Congress is a living hell compared to ten years ago, fifteen years ago, twenty years ago, twenty-five years ago, it is ludicrous.
>
> —House Rules Committee Chairman David Dreier (R-Calif.)

It's easy to idealize the relationship Democrats and Republicans enjoyed before the Republicans took power, when Bob Michel played piano happily alongside Tip O'Neill and commuted by car between Illinois and Washington with House Ways and Means Committee Chairman Dan Rostenkowski (D-Ill.). Democrats like to reminisce about this period when they were in control and the GOP minority relied on the majority's good will for legislative and personal favors. Republicans bridle at this Edenesque depiction of pre-Gingrich Capitol Hill society, considering it more akin to a plantation run by Democrats who were only happy if Republicans accepted a subservient

Epigraphs. David Obey, interview with author, Feb. 10, 2005; David Dreier, interview with author, July 11, 2005.

role in the congressional hierarchy. For their part, Democrats contend that it was the Republicans who deliberately tore apart the Hill's delicate social fabric in order to wrest control of Congress.

The truth is somewhere in between. Republicans and Democrats did get along better before Jim Wright became Speaker, in part because the intensity of national political conflict dipped between Watergate and Ronald Reagan's ascendancy. And Gingrich and his deputies did transform the Hill's social network by urging junior members to keep their families at home in their districts rather than bring them to Washington. But House Democrats also helped poison the well over the past decade, by pursuing ethics claims against Gingrich and feuding over the appointment of the House chaplain in 1999. These scuffles, which the press rarely revisits, sowed distrust between the two parties almost as much as the Republican drive to impeach President Clinton.

In addition, broad institutional changes—members spend less time on the floor debating each other, and more time back home catering to constituents—have eroded the bonds that used to foster comity on Capitol Hill. Lawmakers from opposing parties don't travel together abroad as often, and they no longer frequent the same Washington cocktail parties.

Those are rituals belonging to a distant, more elitist era where a coterie of powerful "wise men" ruled the city, forging backroom deals that defused political tensions but often ignored the public. Lacking any real personal connection to politicians across the aisle, representatives now tend to demonize their opponents rather than engage in genuine policy negotiations. On one level, lawmakers are more focused on their individual constituencies than they used to be. But in the process they have lost touch with one another.

When it comes to civility, the name Barney Frank (D-Mass.) does not immediately leap to mind. Since taking office in 1981, the fiercely liberal congressman has earned a reputation for his sharp tongue, which he freely displays while ripping into his Republican adversaries.

During the impeachment proceedings he was an articulate and passionate defender of President Clinton, and he was one of the first Democrats to use procedural tactics to attack the newly installed GOP majority after 1995.

But Frank is also an institutionalist. He has made his career in the House and has no immediate plans to leave. He has devoted considerable time over the years to befriending both Republicans and Democrats, knowing that he can be most effective if he can assemble an array of legislative coalitions.

"I used to pride myself on knowing all the members," Frank said. "Increasingly I don't get to know the Republicans."[1]

Frank walks into the Members' dining room at lunchtime and now sees tables divided into Democrats and Republicans; inevitably he sits with members of his own party. Much of Capitol Hill is like this now, the product of lawmakers' truncated voting schedule, their aversion to being associated with an "inside-the-Beltway" culture, and their increased suspicion of those on the other side of the aisle.

When lawmakers try to summon up examples of bipartisan bonding, it's usually a stretch. In a 2004 *Vanity Fair* profile Tom DeLay identified Democratic Senator Chuck Schumer (New York) and Sherrod Brown as two Democratic members with whom he's on friendly terms, since they all work out in the same House gym.[2] Brown scoffed at this description, saying the only connection he and the majority leader share is their workout location. "The most substantive conversation we've ever had is 'What time do we get out tonight?'" Brown said. "Here are two of the people he 'works with,' whom he doesn't even know."[3]

1. Barney Frank, interview with author, Feb. 18, 2005.
2. Sam Tannenhaus, "Tom DeLay's Hard Drive," *Vanity Fair*, July 2004.
3. Brown interview. DeLay has had more extensive conversations with Chuck Schumer, whose father was an exterminator just as DeLay was, and whose House gym locker is close to DeLay's, according to an interview the senator gave to reporter Mark Leibovich for his piece, "The Senator Has the Floor; Does Chuck Schumer Have a Story For You!" *The Washington Post*, Aug. 15, 2005.

Thirty years ago, new members were more likely to move their families to D.C. after an election. They were eager to become part of the capital's social scene and wanted their spouses and children near to where they spent most of their week. Families often socialized with each other regardless of party, and these personal ties curbed members' tendency to demonize each other. If Wisconsin Democrat David Obey attacked Representative Willis Gradison (R-Ohio) on the House floor, his wife Jane would lambaste him at home, pointing out that they were likely to have dinner with the Gradisons later in the week.[4]

This sort of lifestyle disappeared in the late 1980s and early 1990s when GOP firebrands like Dick Armey declared themselves members of the "Tuesday to Thursday Club" and spent as little time as possible in Washington. They chose to sleep in their offices rather than waste money on a proper apartment, and they sharply questioned why their colleagues would relocate to the nation's capital. Just a few decades before this, the moniker "Tuesday to Thursday congressman" was an insult that implied the person in question was not a serious legislator. But Armey and Gingrich turned it into a badge of honor, warning the Class of 1994 to keep their families away from D.C.

"You don't want to have your marginal members having a great two years on their way to defeat," Gingrich said, recalling several members of the Senate's GOP Class of 1980 who lost their reelection bids six years later. "It's a reminder when you arrive in a tidal wave, you better train people to build boats. And the boat's called your district."[5]

The growing number of female House members also had an incentive to remain in their districts: many had husbands with established careers back home who did not want to move to Washington. As a result, more lawmakers from both parties began to stay put. A

4. Obey interview.
5. Gingrich interview.

Washington Post survey of forty-two lawmakers in 2001 found only six whose families had permanent addresses in D.C.[6] According to Public Governance Institute President Jerome Climer, who has studied Congress for more than three decades, more than two-thirds of congressional spouses now live outside Washington. Twenty years ago, the figure was less than one-fifth.[7] House Republicans have also devised a schedule so that lawmakers don't need to show up on the Hill as much as they had to in the past: the 108th Congress spent 243 days in session over two years, the fewest since the GOP takeover of the House.[8]

Representative Heather Wilson (R-N.Mex.), who has served in the House since June 1998, is typical. Her family remains in Albuquerque while Wilson shuttles between her district and D.C., where for $600 a month she rents a basement apartment with a beanbag chair and a hook from which she can hang her carry-on luggage. She noted in an interview the House is only supposed to be in session ninety-four days in 2005—"I count these things"—and said she would not consider moving her family from New Mexico: "That's where my life is, and that's where my constituents are."[9]

At the same time members started rushing to catch their Thursday flights back home, they began shunning congressional trips abroad that have traditionally provided another avenue for bipartisan bonding. The media attacked these international and domestic forays as junkets, where either taxpayers or lobbyists paid for politicians and their wives to go on shopping sprees. Sometimes the criticism was justified; at other times it was not. But many lawmakers became wary, fearing they could not convince their constituents that such trips

6. Juliet Eilperin, "Looking Homeward: Many in Congress Choose Commuting," *The Washington Post*, Sept. 3, 2001.

7. Jerome Climer, interview with author, July 8, 2005.

8. The House Rules Committee Minority Office, "Broken Promises: The Death of Deliberative Democracy, A Congressional Report on the Unprecedented Erosion of the Democratic Process in the 108th Congress," Mar. 8, 2005.

9. Heather Wilson, interview with author, July 12, 2005.

helped them do their job. (In fact thirty-five-year veteran GOP Illinois Representative Philip Crane lost his seat in 2004 in part because his opponent capitalized on a National Public Radio report showing Crane had taken fifteen lobbyist-funded trips since 2000 to places like Barbados, Boca Raton, Rome, and Las Vegas, at a total cost of $109,000.)[10] Even official congressional delegations known as CODELs became politicized. When Congressional Indian Caucus Co-chair Joseph Crowley (D-N.Y.) suggested a bipartisan trip to Delhi and Hyderabad in 2003, his GOP counterpart, Joe Wilson (South Carolina), opted for a Republican-only delegation. Crowley ended up shepherding about fifteen Democrats to India during the 108th Congress; Wilson eventually decided not to lead a similar Republican trip.[11]

The few lawmakers who defy this conventional wisdom are among the best at cultivating bipartisan ties on the Hill. Representative Mike Thompson (D-Calif.) spent roughly five days touring Alaska with the state's sole representative, Don Young (R); in 2005 Young affectionately slapped Thompson as they walked down the halls of Congress and told him, "You're one of the good guys."[12] On another occasion conservative talk radio hosts attacked Thompson for visiting Iraq shortly before the U.S. invasion. Representative Mark Foley (R-Fla.), whom Thompson had befriended on a separate trip, took to the air to defend him, pointing out the Californian had served a tour of duty in Vietnam.[13]

A few years ago Representative Chet Edwards (D-Tex.) decided to move his wife and two young children to McLean, Virginia, so he could spend more time with them. Now one of his sons is in the Cub Scouts with Representative Jim McCrery's (R-La.) son, and at

10. Melissa Bean for Congress press release, Sept. 30, 2004.

11. Joseph Crowley and aide to Joe Wilson, interviews with author, Mar. 15 and Mar. 16, 2005.

12. Mike Thompson, interview with author, Feb. 7, 2005.

13. Ibid.

a 2005 White House picnic the two boys spotted each other. As their children approached each other, the two lawmakers decided to dine together and now, Edwards said, "You will never find me going to the floor to criticize the father of my children's friend."[14]

But these kinds of exchanges are the exception, not the rule, in the modern-day Congress.

Members not only stopped sharing free time together over the past decade, they found themselves debating each other less often on the House floor. As with most institutional reforms that have fostered polarization in recent years, Democrats initiated this change, and then Republicans promoted it even more aggressively.

Eager to control the political process and streamline the House schedule, Democratic leaders largely abandoned the "five-minute rule," dividing a set amount of time between the two parties instead of allowing lawmakers from both sides to extend debate by "striking the last word." This both gave party leaders more control—they doled out time to members they preferred, effectively freezing out rebellious ones—and changed the focus of floor debates. By limiting lawmakers to two-minute speeches, leaders stifled opportunities for real debate and encouraged pithy, partisan attacks.

"It's the difference between thirty-minute T.V. shows and thirty-second spots. Which gives you more information?" said Barney Frank, who remembers when he and his colleagues engaged in lengthy floor discussions on everything from defense spending to D.C.'s annual budget. "What can you do in two minutes? Insult the other guy."[15]

A typical House floor debate now is more Kabuki theater than genuine discussion. Lawmakers line up on their respective sides of the aisle and speak behind a podium, gazing at the C-SPAN cameras rather than at their opponents (or even their supporters). Most prepare their speeches in advance so that members are not debating but

14. Chet Edwards, interview with author, June 16, 2005.
15. Frank interview.

speaking past each other in a chamber that is largely empty. When lawmakers actually gather to listen to a major floor debate, they almost always sit with members of their own party.

"Bottom line, the big picture is there are a hundred Republicans who never talk to Democrats on the floor, and a hundred Democrats who never talk to Republicans on the floor," said Collin Peterson (D-Minn.), one of the rare members who often sits on the opposite side of the chamber and breaks ranks with his party on high-profile issues. "They don't know each other, they don't like each other, and they don't trust each other."[16]

In this new climate, politicians have an easier time characterizing one another as devious, ignorant, or dangerous. While U.S. lawmakers have slung mud at one another for more than two centuries—President Andrew Jackson's rivals suggested his mother was a prostitute—political epithets now abound in the House. In the mid-1980s Tip O'Neill called Gingrich, Bob Walker, and Vin Weber "the three stooges."[17] A few years earlier O'Neill was himself the target of twenty-seven-year-old freshman Representative John LeBoutillier (R-N.Y.), who declared the Speaker was "big, fat and out of control—just like the federal government."[18]

Those were the mellow days, before Gingrich gave his troops talking points on how to describe Congress and its Democratic leaders as decaying and corrupt, before New York Representative Charlie Rangel (D-N.Y.) said Gingrich and other backers of the Contract with America were "worse than Hitler,"[19] and his Republican counterpart on the House Ways and Means Committee was "a Nazi."[20] It was

16. Collin Peterson, interview with author, Mar. 10, 2005.

17. Peter Carlson, "Is Bob Walker the Most Obnoxious Man in Congress: It's a Terrible Job, but Somebody's Got to Do It," *The Washington Post Magazine*, Sept. 7, 1986.

18. Chris Vaughan, "Young Congressman Blasts House Speaker," *Associated Press*, July 11, 1981.

19. Michele Parente, "Rangel Ties GOP Agenda to Hitler," *Newsday*, Feb. 19, 1995.

20. Robert Dodge, "Still Focused on Change: With Retirement Approaching, Congressman Bill Archer Continues to Try to Overhaul Social Security, Tax System," *Dallas Morning News*, Oct. 10, 1999.

before another Ways and Means Committee Democrat, Fortney "Pete" Stark (California), called GOP Representative Scott McInnis (Colorado) "a little wimp. . . . You little fruitcake. You little fruitcake. I said you are a fruitcake."[21] After that exchange, Ways and Means Committee Chairman William M. Thomas (R-Calif.) summoned the Capitol police to evict congressional Democrats from the panel's library. Less than a week later, Thomas tearfully apologized for his "poor judgment" on the House floor,[22] but he later blamed the Democrats for provoking him by occupying a room reserved for Republicans and threatening to burst into the committee. "I was concerned about public order," he said in an interview.[23]

Washington politics has reached the point at which name-calling offers tremendous rewards and minimal cost, encouraging lawmakers on both sides to engage in it. Former Representative W. J. "Billy" Tauzin (R-La.) learned this in early 2004, when the Pharmaceutical Manufacturers of America (PhRMA) began courting him to take over the trade association. House Democrats were furious at the idea that Tauzin, who chaired the House Energy and Commerce Committee at the time, would consider retiring to represent an industry he oversaw in Congress. Just a few months before, the GOP had passed its Medicare prescription drug bill, a clear boon to the pharmaceutical industry. Tauzin must have been negotiating behind the scenes with the drug industry, Democrats suggested, even as he was helping write the landmark legislation.

Tauzin, who had served as a Democrat before switching parties in 1995, was equally incensed because the group had only approached him in 2004. Hoping to quell the rumors, he called

21. Juliet Eilperin and Albert B. Crenshaw, "The House that Roared: In Ways and Means Brawl, Names, Police and Sergeant at Arms Are Called," *The Washington Post*, July 19, 2003.

22. Juliet Eilperin, "Ways and Means Chairman Apologizes to House," *The Washington Post*, July 24, 2003.

23. William M. Thomas, interview with author, Mar. 27, 2005.

Nancy Pelosi in late January to request a meeting. The minority leader was heading to the House floor for a vote by the time Tauzin reached her, so she suggested they meet in the chamber to discuss the matter.

Pelosi came over to the Republican side of the aisle to chat with Tauzin as their colleagues milled around them. The Louisiana congressman offered to show her documents detailing the negotiations between his lawyers and the trade association, all of which backed his claim that he did not start talks with the drug industry until after Congress had passed the Medicare bill. Tauzin and Pelosi now offer different accounts of the conversation.

"I don't need to see them," Pelosi said, according to Tauzin.

"So you know it's not true?" Tauzin asked the minority leader.

"I know it's not true," she replied. "Some of my people believe it."

Relieved, Tauzin asked Pelosi if she could muzzle the Democrats questioning his integrity. She was noncommittal.[24]

Pelosi, according to her aides, never said she believed Tauzin's side of the story, and did not promise to remain quiet. Instead, they say, she expressed concern about Tauzin's ill health because he was undergoing tests for intestinal cancer.[25]

That same afternoon, Pelosi gave a speech in which she suggested Tauzin had made a secret deal with pharmaceutical companies in the hopes of becoming their trade association's president. "Seniors who are wondering why the pharmaceutical companies made out so well in this bill at their expense, need only to look at this example of abuse of power and conflict of interest," she said at a news conference. "I think it would be important to the American people to know when the negotiations for these positions began."[26]

Within a matter of hours, the minority leader had launched a political attack that eviscerated the informal relationship she had

24. W. J. "Billy" Tauzin, interview with author, July 18, 2005.
25. Aides to Nancy Pelosi, interview with author, July 22, 2005.
26. Ted Barrett, "Pelosi Rips GOP Lawmaker on Job Offer," CNN.com, Jan. 28, 2004.

enjoyed with Tauzin for roughly two decades. When Tauzin entered the hospital the next month to seek treatment for cancer, Pelosi sent him a bouquet of flowers. But the gesture failed to move him.

"I could never trust Nancy Pelosi again in my life," said Tauzin, who ultimately took the PhRMA job. "It tears down the capacity of an institution to work."[27]

A series of concrete actions over the past decade accompanied this bitter rhetoric, further eroding relations between the two parties. Once Gingrich became speaker, Democrats launched a broad campaign to discredit him both within the House and on the public airwaves; Gingrich estimates that from 1995 to 1996 his opponents aired 123,000 negative ads against him,[28] besides filing an array of ethics charges alleging he violated House rules. House GOP leaders, for their part, froze out Gephardt from the legislative process on the grounds that he couldn't aid them legislatively and couldn't be trusted.

"You could not attempt to appease the Democrats because the price they would charge for appeasement was too high," Gingrich said, adding that when it came to Gephardt, "Why would you go to somebody who you believed couldn't deliver, couldn't be counted on and wouldn't tell you the truth?"[29]

Within a month of taking over the majority, Gingrich and his staff decided it was pointless to engage in discussions with Gephardt on any policy issue, domestic or foreign, despite the nation's long history of bipartisanship on foreign affairs.

House Democrats also had little interest in collaborating. With just a handful of seats separating them from reclaiming the majority, Democrats cared more about defining their differences with their

27. Tauzin interview.
28. Gingrich interview.
29. Ibid.

GOP counterparts than striking legislative deals. "In those three elections—1996, 1998 and 2000, when we believed we had a significant chance to win—we thought we were fighting the war to end all wars and it was not in our interest to get things done," said Steve Elmendorf, who served as Gephardt's chief of staff until December 2002. "It contributed to the institution's problems."[30]

Occasionally it looked as if the two parties could get past this strategy, but these opportunities evaporated rapidly. When in December 1998 Speaker-designate Bob Livingston announced during the final impeachment debate that he would resign in light of press reports that he had cheated on his wife, Gephardt tore up his prepared speech and pleaded with his colleagues to make a fresh start in the House.

"We need to start healing. We need to start binding up our wounds," Gephardt said. "We need to end this downward spiral which will culminate in the death of representative democracy. . . . We are on the brink of the abyss. The only way we can stop this insanity is through the force of our own will."[31] (Full text on pages 145–46.)

But the Republicans went ahead and approved two articles of impeachment against President Clinton that day, with just a small number of Republicans breaking ranks on a couple of charges. Livingston gave up his seat, and Dennis Hastert took the helm of the House. The "politics of personal destruction" that Gephardt had alluded to in his floor speech remained alive and well in Washington.

At first, some Democrats and Republicans thought Hastert represented a fresh start, a leader who could soothe the partisan tensions that impeachment had inflamed. The new Speaker was something of a mystery to Democrats, an unassuming former wrestling coach and high school teacher from the Midwest who had shown little personal

30. Steve Elmendorf, interview with author, Jan. 17, 2005.

31. *Congressional Record*, Dec. 19, 1998.

ambition since winning national office in 1986. He had a solid conservative voting record and cared about health care and the drug war in Colombia, but displayed no affinity for the kind of high-stakes political gamesmanship that Gingrich reveled in during his tenure as Speaker. And no one could question his personal affability; Hastert is an unpretentious bear of a man with a ready smile. He ambles through the corridors of the Capitol at a leisurely pace even when under intense political pressure. On taking office Hastert declared, "I think we should agree that stalemate is not an option, solutions are."[32]

But for much of Hastert's first year the parties continued their war over contentious political issues, sparring over gun control and whether to authorize force in NATO's air campaign over Kosovo. Democrats started questioning his leadership on April 28, 1999, when the House voted 213 to 213 to reject the Senate-passed resolution authorizing NATO's five-week-old air campaign in the Balkans. While Hastert supported the resolution, he sat quietly in the chamber, letting then-House Majority Whip Tom DeLay convince all but thirty-one Republicans to oppose—and thus kill—the bill.[33] After that, Democrats concluded there was little point in reaching out to the Speaker.

No one, however, was prepared for the firestorm of controversy that would erupt late in 1999 when House leaders had to determine who would take over for the Reverend James D. Ford, a popular Lutheran who had served for two decades as the chamber's chaplain. Hastert had established an unprecedented bipartisan panel of nine Republicans and nine Democrats to select a successor. They spent more than three months winnowing down a list of forty candidates to three finalists. Catholic priest Tim O'Brien, who at the time directed the Marquette University Les Aspin Center for Government, received the most votes from the bipartisan group, with the Reverend

32. Eric Pianin and Juliet Eilperin, "No Love Lost for Hastert, Gephardt; Bitter Relations Add to House Gridlock," *The Washington Post*, Mar. 20, 2000.
33. Ibid.

Robert Dvorak, superintendent of the East Coast Conference of the Evangelical Covenant Church, coming in second. The Reverend Charles Parker Wright, a Presbyterian, received the fewest votes.

The top three House leaders—Hastert, Armey, and Gephardt—interviewed the finalists to choose Ford's successor. Gephardt backed O'Brien while Hastert and Armey found Wright, who headed the National Prayer Breakfast, more empathetic. While Gephardt expressed frustration at the result—telling Hastert in a private meeting, "If you were going to do this, why didn't you just do it in the beginning?"—he signed off on a letter announcing Wright's appointment.[34]

The leaders' agreement did not settle the matter, however. Members of the bipartisan panel such as Anna G. Eshoo (D-Calif.), a Catholic, questioned why the two Republicans had bypassed O'Brien. "I don't think the entire thing is an anti-Catholic bias," she told *The Washington Post*. "Do I think that's part of it? I do."[35]

Hastert and Armey, both evangelicals, were furious. They bristled at the idea that they could be prejudiced and resented Gephardt, who had technically agreed to Wright's appointment, for doing nothing to quiet his troops. At one point during the crisis Hastert found himself sitting late at night in his office with his closest advisers: lobbyist Dan Mattoon and aides Scott Palmer, Mike Stokke, and John Feehery. Aside from Hastert, Palmer was the only non-Catholic in the room. "I've got Catholics surrounding me here," Hastert quipped.[36]

While Hastert could joke with his own staff, the incident soured him on Gephardt for good. Using his connections to Chicago's Cardinal Francis George, the speaker found Daniel Coughlin, a Catholic vicar in Chicago whom he interviewed on his own. On March 23,

34. Gephardt interview.

35. Juliet Eilperin, "Appointment of Chaplain Splits House," *The Washington Post*, Dec. 3, 1999.

36. One of Hastert's top advisers who asked not to be identified, interview with author, Mar. 31, 2005.

2000, Hastert introduced Coughlin to his colleagues in a blistering speech on the House floor, during which he likened the chaplain dispute to "war. And it has an ugly face."

"I am a patient man. In my role as Speaker of the whole House, I believe I should try to be especially patient, and seek compromise and not confrontation. But even I do not easily take in stride carelessly tossed accusations of bigotry," Hastert said in the speech. "Where I come from, such slander is an ugly business. I can only conclude that those who accuse me of anti-Catholic bigotry either don't know me or are maliciously seeking political advantage by making these accusations. . . . And it is with that conviction that I say to each of you that I believe the political maneuvering on this issue may have catastrophic unintended consequences, like children playing with matches."[37] (Full text on pages 147–52.)

To this day, Hastert and Armey harbor resentment stemming from the chaplain controversy. In his recent book, *Speaker: Lessons from Forty Years in Coaching and Politics*, Hastert mocked Gephardt for insisting he had to "check with my people" before saying which chaplain candidate he would back. "That's what he always said. He seldom made a decision on his own."[38] Hastert added that when it came to his Democratic counterpart, "after that, I never expected much from him."[39]

Armey, one of whose sons has converted to Catholicism, called the incident "mean as spit. . . . I was as angry as I could be. It should have been beneath the dignity of any eighth-grader to do this kind of garbage."[40]

The dispute had practical implications, as well as psychological ones. Hastert had been preparing to reestablish a bipartisan task force

37. *Congressional Record*, Mar. 23, 2000.

38. Denny Hastert, *Speaker: Lessons from Forty Years in Coaching and Politics* (Washington, D.C.: Regnery Publishing, 2004), 201.

39. Ibid, 206.

40. Armey interview.

on drug policy, one of his most cherished legislative priorities. After the chaplain incident he informed Representative Mark Souder (Indiana), the task force's Republican co-chair, that he would no longer put Democrats on the panel. "I can't trust them," Hastert told Souder. "I'm going to create a speaker's drug task force, where I pick Republicans, and then you can go out and make a bipartisan coalition if you want."[41]

The Democrats, for their part, felt equally maligned. "It's the only thing they did on a bipartisan basis in ten years and they screwed that up, and we're the offenders," said one House Democratic leadership aide who asked not to be identified. "It's absurd."[42]

Gephardt said he knew at the time the rift had damaged his relationship with the Speaker—"It made it hard after that, I felt he had lost faith in me," he said—but he also felt that Hastert had bungled the rare foray into bipartisanship. "We couldn't even do that. It was maddening, it was frustrating," Gephardt said.[43]

Democrats don't tend to think much about the chaplain incident, in the same way that Republicans forget how their impeachment of President Clinton infuriated the House's minority party. New York Representative Steve Israel, a moderate Democrat who has started the "Center Aisle Caucus" along with Representative Timothy V. Johnson (R-Ind.), to restore civility to the House, said some of his colleagues refuse to join because they remain scarred by the impeachment drive: "Many members said, 'We shouldn't do it because of what they did to us.' They saw what [Republicans] had done to Clinton, and now it's O.K. to do it to everybody."[44] Each side nurses its own

41. Mark Souder, interview with author, July 21, 2005.

42. House leadership aide who asked not to be identified, interview with author, Mar. 3, 2005.

43. Gephardt interview.

44. Steve Israel, interview with author, Mar. 10, 2005.

wounds, ignoring how its political barbs and harsh tactics can alienate members from the opposing party.

Armey's attitude toward House Democrats highlights this sort of contradiction. Four of his five best friends from his time serving in Congress are Democrats, he said, because he didn't have to jockey with them for a party leadership position. But in the same interview he blamed the minority for the current tension on Capitol Hill: "The lack of civility begins with the Democrats. They have a notion we are inferior people."[45]

He thinks just as dimly of his opponents, saying that Hastert was more disillusioned by the chaplain controversy than he was because "I had long since concluded Democrats are no damn good."[46]

45. Armey interview.
46. Ibid.

CHAPTER 3

Legislating without a Partnership

At some point, you have to accept the fact [Democrats] have voluntarily chosen to remove themselves from the interactive aspect of the legislative process. Does that mean you don't legislate? Of course not. . . . If I turned the committee over to them, they would be happy to legislate. That's the only way they would participate. And I can't let them have the committee, so that's where we are.

—House Ways and Means Committee
Chairman William M. Thomas (R-Calif.)

You're going to love this job, you don't have to do anything.

—A senior California Republican speaking to
Democratic Representative Mike Thompson
upon his arrival in Washington

In the spring of 2005, the House Judiciary Committee took up a constitutional amendment, written by Representative Brian Baird (D-Wash.), which was aimed at addressing the problem of how to respond if large numbers of members died or became incapacitated in a terrorist attack or disaster. The measure would have called for "alternates" to be elected every two years so that if a lawmaker died, an elected representative could take his or her place.

On its face the question of how to preserve a working House in the face of disaster seems like a nonpartisan issue, since it speaks to the institution's overall survival rather than to one party's advantage. But House Judiciary Committee Chairman F. James Sensenbrenner

Epigraphs. Thomas interview; Thompson interview.

Jr. (R-Wis.) opposed Baird's bill: he had his own version that would call on states to hold special elections within forty-nine days if one hundred or more House members died or became incapacitated. Sensenbrenner refused to let Baird speak on his alternative when it came up for a committee vote.

"Common courtesy would say if you're discussing someone's bill you ought to let him speak on it," Baird said. "It is cowardice and bullying to do otherwise."[1]

Baird's bill lost badly in committee, while Sensenbrenner's proposal eventually made it through the House by a margin of 329 to 68. Judiciary Committee spokesman Jeff Lungren said the panel held "a full and open debate" on the subject.

"He just makes ridiculous arguments about how this issue has been handled," Lungren said of Baird. "He's not a member of the committee."[2]

Analyzing how House Democrats got shut out of the legislative process raises the chicken and the egg problem. Democrats say Republicans deliberately excluded them from lawmaking once they took control of the chamber in 1995. Republicans counter that Democrats have shown little interest in cutting the kind of deals they were willing to strike when the Democrats ruled the House. Even many House Republicans will acknowledge much of the impasse stems from their approach. Rather than seeking a comfortable bipartisan majority for their initiatives, GOP leaders are more interested in securing 218 votes on their side, so they can craft bills that are as conservative as possible. Democratic support after the fact is welcomed, but not essential, since Republicans want to counterbalance the more moderate Senate. In an interview in late 2003, House Majority Whip Roy Blunt's (R-Mo.) director of floor operations, Amy

1. Brian Baird, interview with author, June 25, 2005.
2. Jeff Lungren, interview with author, July 1, 2005.

Steinmann, said that when it came to Democrats, "for my purposes, they're irrelevant."[3]

With such a slim margin separating the parties, Republicans argue, the GOP is best off marshalling support for legislation on its own. And the House has always been a majoritarian institution, where the party in control imposes its vision on the chamber.

This strategy has encouraged Democrats to become even more partisan, however, because they have nothing invested in the measures Hastert brings to the House floor. It has also prompted GOP leaders to rush through legislation with little oversight, short-circuiting the public debate that often exposes a bill's potential flaws.

The House has begun to resemble a parliamentary system, with each side trying to win over voters by offering distinct agendas. In a press conference in April 2005, Nancy Pelosi explained that Democrats want to "differentiate" themselves from the GOP in Americans' minds. Her party, she said, "will make it very clear to the American people, because they don't know, it just doesn't get through to them, and sometimes despite your best efforts to spell out the differences for them, it just doesn't get through to them. So we have to do a better job, a more dramatic job of differentiating and, in doing so, also to put forth a positive agenda, which we have done with our New Partnership for America's Future."[4] Between the time she took power and the end of the 108th Congress, Pelosi noted, House Democrats were more unified on floor votes than at any time since 1960, when the legendary House Speaker Sam Rayburn (D-Tex.) ruled the chamber.[5]

On a certain level this strategy of highlighting the parties' policy differences seems reasonable. For years, lines between Republicans and Democrats were blurred; now voters have a better sense of where

3. Juliet Eilperin, "House GOP Practices Act of One-Vote Victories," *The Washington Post*, Oct. 14, 2003.

4. Transcript of Nancy Pelosi's weekly press conference, Apr. 6, 2005.

5. Daly interview.

lawmakers stand. "Pre-'94 you couldn't distinguish between the parties' platforms because they didn't mean anything," Bill Paxon said. "I would think our Founding Fathers would think this is a good thing. . . . They wanted real debate over real issues."[6] Or as Princeton University political scientist Larry Bartels observed, academics in his field spent years calling on Democrats and Republicans to be more cohesive as parties. "Now we have responsive party government, all the political scientists spend their time whining about what a disaster it is," he said.[7]

The parliamentary approach to legislating, however, ignores some fundamental problems. Redistricting has made it so difficult to unseat incumbents that even if voters become outraged and want to oust the majority—the "throw the bums out" scenario—they would have a hard time doing so. "It's a combination of having a huge number of non-competitive districts in the country and a huge partisan bias that's deadly," said Sam Hirsch, an attorney at the firm Jenner & Block who represented House Democrats in several of their redistricting legal challenges after 2000. "It's really about making sure control of the body is up for grabs, depending on how public opinion shifts and how the parties do their politics. And it's not.[8]

Just as important, this approach to legislating has made it difficult to achieve the kind of bipartisan compromises that have wrought landmark legislative achievements for decades. Moreover when one party—here the House Democrats—represents slightly less than half of the American public and are shut out from drafting laws, their constituents lose the opportunity to influence national policy. And even Bill Thomas (R-Calif.)—whose hard-edged tactics have angered Democrats repeatedly over the years—said he wants to collaborate more closely with the minority.

"Is it as good legislation as I could have made if we had a working

6. Paxon interview.
7. Larry Bartels, interview with author, Feb. 25, 2005.
8. Sam Hirsch, interview with author, Jan. 19, 2005.

relationship? Of course not," he said. "I can't get [Democrats] to participate as junior partners. It has to be totally hostile so they can complain we're being unfair."[9]

One of the best ways to gauge the ability of the minority to influence legislation in the House is to examine the chamber's rules process. This system, which is determined by the GOP-dominated Rules Committee, establishes the guidelines for floor debate and the amendments that can be offered to pending legislation. The Rules Committee decides what kind of changes lawmakers can offer to bills once they reach the floor, and how long members can discuss them. While this ranks as one of the House's least decipherable aspects to outside observers, it has a huge impact on what kinds of policies emerge from the House. An amendment may enjoy broad bipartisan support, for example, but if the Rules Committee decides it is out of order, it will never have a shot on the House floor.

When Democrats ruled the chamber, Republicans spoke at length about the need for "open rules"—where any member can offer a relevant amendment to legislation. David Dreier (R-Calif.), who now crafts these terms of debate as chair of the House Rules Committee, said in 1993, "While the majority party always has the right to establish the rules and legislative agenda for the House, it should recognize the need to place responsible limits on those powers which permit all members to fully participate in a truly deliberative process and of all the people to be fully represented in their national legislature."[10] His fellow panel member Lincoln Diaz-Balart (R-Fla.) lambasted the idea of limiting amendments a couple of weeks later on the House floor, saying, "The American people have got to find out about it, they have got to put pressures on the leadership of this institution to undo and do away once and for all with that most

9. Thomas interview.

10. *Congressional Record*, Apr. 21, 1993.

undemocratic principle, most undemocratic practice called and known as the infamous closed rule."[11]

As with many of the trends toward polarization on Capitol Hill, closed rules—where no amendments can be offered to a bill—began under the Democrats. In the 1980s, worried about Democratic defections and about resistance from members who were chafing at spending such long hours in Washington, Speakers O'Neill, Wright, and Foley started restricting lawmakers' ability to offer amendments on the House floor. By the 103rd Congress 70 percent of all rules were either restricted or completely closed. When Republicans took over in the 104th Congress, House Rules Committee Chairman Gerald B. H. Solomon (R-N.Y.) vowed to have "70 percent open and unrestricted rules, if we possibly can."[12]

The House Republicans never lived up to that promise. While Solomon apparently fought behind the scenes for open rules, GOP leaders have reported an increasing number of closed rules over time since taking the majority. In the 108th Congress, just 22 percent of the rules reported out by the House Rules Committee were open, the lowest percentage since the GOP won control of the House.[13] House Rules Committee Democrats issued a report on this phenomenon in March 2005 in which they called Republicans "the most arrogant, unethical and corrupt majority in modern congressional history . . . what sets the 108th Congress apart from its predecessors is that stifling deliberation and quashing dissent in the House of Representatives became the standard operating procedure."[14]

House GOP leaders say they have no choice but to adopt a hard line, because of their narrow margin of control. Obtaining the necessary 218 votes, culled almost entirely from within the Republican

11. *Congressional Record*, Mar. 3, 1993.

12. *Congressional Record*, Jan. 5, 1995.

13. House Rules Committee Minority Office, "Broken Promises: The Death of Deliberative Democracy," 12.

14. Ibid, 4.

Conference, means striking several complicated deals that a single amendment could derail. That's a risk they're not willing to take.

"If we had 70 votes or 110 votes to spare, don't you think we'd make open rules?" Thomas asked. "When you have five or 12 votes to spare you have to utilize the tools available to the majority."[15]

Dreier said he did not realize before taking power why the majority needs to use restrictive tactics on occasion, and now he does. But he also sees his panel's job as "to move the speaker's agenda in the fairest, most balanced way possible," and describes the GOP's overarching mission as "to pursue the best public policy possible, to be deliberative, to allow a wide range of views to be considered, and to follow what we see as constitutional government."[16]

Most Democrats question whether Dreier's description of the current rules process reflects reality. When the House Financial Services Committee took up legislation in 2005 affecting the lending institutions Fannie Mae and Freddie Mac, Barney Frank offered an amendment calling for the two organizations to devote 5 percent of their after-tax profits to creating affordable housing. The amendment passed fifty-three to seventeen, with more than a dozen Republicans joining all of the panel's Democrats in support. But GOP conservatives appealed directly to their leaders, urging them to scuttle the amendment once the bill reached the Rules Committee. After weeks of talks, the two sides agreed to a proposal by conservatives that barred any group participating in election activities from applying for the funds. But conservatives also inserted language barring any group whose primary mission was not providing housing, which disqualified both some liberal groups and most religious organizations. Frank tried to offer an amendment striking this provision, but the GOP overruled him; the bill passed in late October despite his objections.[17]

Some Republicans are growing discomfited at the idea of so many

15. Thomas interview.

16. Dreier interview.

17. Steve Adamske, interview with the author, Dec. 1, 2005.

restrictions on members' ability to alter legislation on the House floor. "Here we are fighting for democracy in Iraq and Afghanistan and we have more and more closed rules here," said Representative Gil Gutknecht (R-Minn.). "We don't want democracy to flourish on the floor of the House of Representatives."[18]

Democrats are now making the same argument their GOP predecessors made in the early 1990s, which is that by blocking the minority from offering amendments, the majority is silencing a large number of Americans. "When they shut down the Democrats, they are shutting down at least half the people," Pelosi said in the spring of 2005. "They are shutting down many minorities; they are shutting down the diversity of our country. It is a losing proposition for our country because this diversity of opinion is what we were all about to begin with."[19]

Democrats have borne the brunt of the leadership's rules policy. They offered twenty-nine amendments to a medical malpractice bill during the 108th Congress, and the Republicans denied all of them. That same Congress they proposed thirty-six amendments to the Medicare prescription drug bill, of which the Republicans allowed one. The bankruptcy bill offers a case study of how GOP leaders have become more restrictive over time. During the 105th Congress they allowed twelve amendments on the floor. By the 109th Congress they allowed none on a nearly identical bill.[20] This "take it or leave it" policy offers Democrats a difficult choice: either accept the Republicans' policy vision or walk away from the bill altogether.

Sometimes GOP leaders have blocked their own members from tinkering with legislation as well. In 2003 James Leach (R-Iowa), who had chaired what is now known as the House Financial Services Committee, tried to amend a banking bill to strengthen federal oversight of lending institutions known as "industrial loan companies."

18. Gil Gutknecht, interview with author, May 2, 2005.
19. Pelosi's Apr. 6, 2005 press conference.
20. "Broken Promises," 19.

The House Rules Committee denied him the opportunity. Leach called the decision "a scandal. I consider it an embarrassment to the House that this issue cannot be debated on the most important banking bill that is going to be debated before this Congress this year."[21]

Other times GOP leaders have deliberately distorted proposals by rank-and-file members out of fear they might pass. Representative Jeff Flake (R-Ariz.), a conservative, became furious in July 2005 after senior Republicans derailed his popular amendment allowing U.S. citizens the right to send personal-hygiene products to relatives in Cuba, by circulating a flier on the floor suggesting the measure would allow "unfettered trade with the communist regime of Cuba with no Administration oversight of said trade."

"I don't mind losing a fair fight," Flake said. "When your own party puts out that kind of garbage it's really troublesome. . . . There's a lot of underlying frustration beginning to bubble up among lawmakers."[22]

By quashing rank-and-file members' proposals, American Enterprise Institute scholar Norman J. Ornstein observed, Republicans are short-circuiting the normal give-and-take that defines a healthy legislative process. "It's not just that it offends me that they're shutting people out," Ornstein said. "It's that you end up with bad legislation."[23]

At the same time that House Republicans have cut back on floor amendments, they have reduced the time members have to review legislation. During the 108th Congress the Rules Committee routinely adopted "emergency" procedures waiving requirements that allow lawmakers at least forty-eight hours to scrutinize bills. Sixty percent of all rules qualified for this emergency treatment, and nearly

21. Ibid, 20.
22. Jeff Flake, interview with author, July 7, 2005.
23. Norman J. Ornstein, interview with author, June 16, 2005.

40 percent of all rules were reported after eight o'clock at night, making it harder for members to examine and propose changes to pending bills before the leadership shepherds the bills to the floor.[24]

"We get this stuff warm off the printer and they ring the bell, and we have fifteen minutes to vote," complained Mike Thompson.[25] In early 2005 House leaders gave Democrats one hour before the floor vote on a three-thousand-page budget bill that was to determine how the federal government would spend $1 trillion in taxpayer dollars over the coming year. Representative Bob Filner (D-Calif.) proposed Democrats take the massive bill outside on the U.S. Capitol steps and begin to read it in order to draw attention to the Republicans' governing tactics. Instead, his colleagues stayed inside to debate the measure.[26]

In fact the Rules Committee—which is already stacked in favor of the majority by a nine to four ratio—has become such a tool of the leadership that ambitious lawmakers are fleeing the panel. Long ago the Rules Committee was an independent power base in the House, where Southern conservatives managed to bottle up progressive legislation. Now it does exactly what the leadership wants, to such an extent that five of the committee's nine Republicans from the 108th Congress left this year. While Representative Porter Goss (R-Fla.) retired, the other four—John Linder (Georgia), Sue Myrick (North Carolina), Deborah Pryce (Ohio), and Thomas Reynolds (New York)—all opted for other assignments in 2005. The Democrats are becoming equally reluctant to serve on the panel. When Martin Frost's defeat opened up a slot on the panel, House Democrats had a hard time filling it.

In such a poisoned atmosphere, Republicans and Democrats have

24. "Broken Promises," 34–35.
25. Thompson interview.
26. Bob Filner, interview with author, May 4, 2005.

taken to using the most obscure of legislative vehicles—committee report language—as a political battleground. While report language matters—when a law is challenged, for example, judges often scrutinize the language accompanying a bill to glean its authors' intent—it rarely rises to the level of public debate. But in April 2005 Representative Jerrold Nadler (D-N.Y.) became outraged when he read how Judiciary Committee Republicans had characterized his proposal to amend the Child Interstate Abortion Notification Act, which would make transporting a minor across state lines to have an abortion a criminal offense. Nadler sought to exclude grandparents and adult siblings of the minor in question from the law; the final committee report suggested such a proposal would "exempt sexual predators" from prosecution and conviction.

Nadler complained before the House Rules Committee, calling the Republican characterization of his amendment "dishonest and dishonoring to the institution." Sensenbrenner, whose aide had written the offending phrase, refused to back down and accused the Democrats of legislative sloppiness. When Democrats offered a motion to criticize the GOP-crafted report language, Republicans set it aside in a party-line vote. After some moderate Republicans privately objected to Sensenbrenner's tactics, House leaders convinced him to submit a supplemental report removing the controversial references.[27]

The public flare-up did not temper Sensenbrenner's behavior, however. A few weeks later he became impatient when Nadler and other committee Democrats started questioning the constitutionality of the USA Patriot Act during a hearing on the anti-terrorism bill; Sensenbrenner abruptly gaveled the hearing to a close, walked out of the room, and ordered the Democrats' microphones shut off. Taken together, the two incidents prompted Brookings Institution scholar

27. Jonathan E. Kaplan, "GOP Leaders Tone Down Sensenbrenner's Words," *Hill*, May 10, 2005.

Thomas E. Mann to dub Sensenbrenner "the most arrogant member of the Republican majority."[28]

Judiciary Committee spokesman Jeff Lungren said Sensenbrenner had already accommodated Democrats on the Patriot Act by allowing them to hold a hearing with only Democratic witnesses, to counterbalance a hearing earlier in the week with Bush's deputy attorney general. While Sensenbrenner acknowledged he adjourned the hearing "in an improper manner," Lungren said, he added that did not justify the Democrats' reaction.

"Nadler wanted an issue," he said. "I think the Democratic leaders wanted it too."[29]

On occasion House Republicans have broken their governing pattern and reached out to Democrats, for example, in drafting President Bush's No Child Left Behind education bill. Upon winning the presidency in 2000, Bush announced his intention to bring the parties together. He saw a major education initiative as the best way to bridge the gap between Democrats and Republicans and brought several key lawmakers down to meet with him in Texas on December 21, 2000, including House Education and Workforce Committee Chairman John Boehner (R-Ohio) and his Democratic counterpart, George Miller. Miller was not on the White House's original invitation list; Boehner insisted that he come, and GOP Senator Judd Gregg (New Hampshire) switched his place card so Miller (California) ended up sitting next to the president-elect at lunch.[30]

In personality and ideology, Boehner and Miller could hardly be more different. Boehner, a perpetually tan, self-made millionaire who made a name for himself in D.C. as a member of the reform-minded

28. Thomas E. Mann, interview with author, June 15, 2005.

29. Lungren interview.

30. David S. Broder, "Long Road to Reform: Negotiators Forge Education Legislation," *The Washington Post*, Dec. 17, 2001.

"Gang of Seven" in the 1990s and now serves as House minority leader, is a solid conservative with close ties to the corporate sector. Miller, nicknamed "Big George" by the president for his considerable height and girth, is an outspoken liberal who has served in Congress for thirty years. As GOP Conference Chairman, by contrast, Boehner headed the "Thursday Group," a setting for lobbyists to brief him each week on issues that mattered to them. Miller led a decade-long battle to salvage the reputation of fifty Port Chicago "Mutineers," black sailors from World War II who refused to resume loading munitions at the Port Chicago Naval Weapons Station in Concord, California, after a mysterious explosion in 1944 killed 320 sailors.[31]

Despite their different philosophical outlooks, both of them cared about public education, and they worked together to craft a compromise measure that could win the backing of a majority of Republicans and Democrats. The bill's basic premise was that schools should receive generous federal funding in exchange for greater accountability in performance, which government officials could gauge through standardized tests. Shortly before the bill was to come to the floor, several conservatives on Boehner's committee insisted that he include a "Straight A's" pilot program giving block grants to states, a provision Democrats saw as a deal-breaker.[32]

Boehner knew he had to kill it, but that meant angering some of his own members as well as top GOP leaders. While he left to play golf in South Carolina with some of his congressional buddies, White House officials began calling him furiously to demand he meet in the Oval Office with Bush along with Hastert, Armey, and DeLay. Upon arriving back in Washington the night before the vote, Boehner's cell phone rang again. He was to get to the White House in fifteen minutes.

31. George Miller's Web site at www.house.gov/georgemiller/bio.html.

32. Democrats thought the provision could undermine some of the basic educational guarantees the federal government sought to ensure through school funding, while Republicans believed it would encourage policy innovation.

Still dressed in his golfing togs, Boehner borrowed a tie from Georgia Republican Saxby Chambliss (now a senator) and a sports coat from Representative Tom Latham (R-Iowa). Boehner rushed into the Oval Office in time to hear DeLay trashing his bill. Armey and Hastert followed with their own barrage of criticisms, arguing it was not conservative enough.

Bush, who had already winked twice at the Ohio Republican during the House leaders' attack, asked Boehner to defend his strategy. A partisan bill, Boehner said, was "a dead-end street." They needed Democratic votes for a large victory that would lend the bill serious credibility with both educators and voters.

Bush looked at the four men and announced, "I'm with Boehner. The meeting's over."[33]

That week the House approved the most sweeping change to federal education policy in nearly four decades by a margin of 384 to 45. All but 34 Republicans, 10 Democrats, and one independent voted aye, though it took another six months before the two chambers could reconcile their competing bills and send legislation to the White House for Bush's signature. Bush declared upon signing the bill that its passage "begins a new era, a new time in public education in our country,"[34] and he and Boehner broke into tears as they embraced at the ceremony.

The legislation angered some House GOP conservatives, and Hastert has told allies privately that the bipartisan compromise was not worth the headaches it created for him in his own ranks. Democrats repaid the Republicans for their cooperation by attacking the program on the campaign trail. Three years later Republicans are still demanding Boehner move further to the right if he wants to advance

33. Republicans familiar with the meeting, who asked not to be identified, interview with author, Feb. 9, 2005.

34. Dana Milbank, "With Fanfare, Bush Signs Education Bill; President, Lawmakers Hit 3 States in 12 Hours to Tout Biggest Schools Change Since '65," *The Washington Post*, Jan. 9, 2002.

politically. Representative Walter B. Jones (R-N.C.) approached Boehner on the House floor in early 2005 and teased him, "When are you going to come back into the fold? If you want to be speaker some day, you've got to come back into the fold."[35]

Boehner is not the only senior House Republican who has come under fire for working with Democrats. One former high-ranking Republican who asked not to be identified said he has sometimes had to deflect criticism from his superiors for trying to craft bipartisan bills.

"Sometimes you are told, as a member of the Republican side, 'Why are you working with Democrats when we can get it passed with Republican votes only?'" he said. "As a member of leadership, now and again you are faced with the decision: Do you do what you think is best for the country and public policy, or do you do what may be best to retain the majority?"[36]

Another senior Republican described his dilemma this way: "The problem we have in Congress is we can't get any help from the Democrats, and we didn't give them any help either. The leadership has decided everything comes with Republican votes. Right now the middle has collapsed in American politics."[37]

After No Child Left Behind, House Republicans rarely again used that kind of bipartisan approach when it came to top-tier legislation. Instead they managed to pass a slew of major bills, including big tax cuts and medical malpractice legislation, on largely party-line votes. The culmination of this strategy came in November 2003 during con-

35. Walter B. Jones, interview with author, Oct. 19, 2005. Jones said that while he would like to see Boehner as Speaker, "what I was saying is John needed to be identified with less government, not more government. . . . No Child Left Behind is an expansion of government."

36. Former senior Republican who asked not to be identified, interview with author, Aug. 31, 2005.

37. Senior Republican who asked not to be identified, interview with author, Oct. 21, 2005.

sideration of Bush's plan to add a prescription drug care benefit to the nation's Medicare system, a bold proposal aimed at overhauling the popular health care program. Liberals didn't like the $400 billion measure, saying it would not cover enough seniors and amounted to a gift to the pharmaceutical industry. Conservatives blanched at the program's price tag, saying it was antithetical to the Republicans' vision of smaller government.

The unprecedented two-hour, fifty-one-minute vote—which lasted from three in the morning until nearly six in the morning—illustrates the broad gulf between Democrats and Republicans in the House today. House votes technically last fifteen minutes, but the majority party decides when a vote actually ends by gaveling it to a close. When Jim Wright once allowed a vote to drag on as long as an hour, Republicans cried foul. Wright's ploy seems tame in comparison with the 2003 Medicare vote.

From the outset, it was clear Republicans had little interest in bringing Democrats into the drafting process. As chairman of the Ways and Means Committee, Thomas brought in Representative Collin Peterson (D-Minn.) for talks because he was confident its provision helping the elderly in rural areas would ensure the centrist Democrat's support. Thomas excluded other potential allies among the moderate Democratic camp. When Representative Marion Berry (D-Ark.) reported back to some of his colleagues on one meeting he attended, Thomas told Peterson that Berry was no longer welcome.[38]

House Republicans used this same approach when assembling negotiators to hammer out the final bill. As chair of the sessions, Thomas included two Senate Democrats who backed aspects of the plan, Max Baucus (Montana) and John Breaux (Louisiana). But he refused to allow two other Senate Finance Committee Democrats—then-Senate Minority Leader Thomas A. Daschle (South Dakota) and Senator John D. Rockefeller IV (West Virginia)—to join the confer-

38. Peterson interview.

ence committee. He also refused membership to Ways and Means Committee ranking member Charlie Rangel (D). "What they're saying is that they will just ram it down our throats," Rangel said.[39] While congressional tradition dictated that the minority party always got to send delegates of its choice to final negotiations on a bill, GOP leaders calculated there was no sense bringing in lawmakers who would try to disrupt the process but who lacked the votes to influence the end product.

Still, this left House Republicans with a serious problem coming into the November floor vote on the final bill. A few months earlier they had passed the House version of the measure by just one vote, and they needed Democratic votes to ensure a victory. Pelosi had relentlessly badgered Democrats to stay the course and oppose the bill, which ranked as one of the president's top legislative priorities for his reelection campaign. Steve Israel, who faced a health crisis in his district as managed-care companies fled Long Island, leaving tens of thousands of senior citizens uninsured, voted for the House bill in the summer of 2003. Pelosi called him into her office for a ten-minute lecture on why he had to reverse his vote when the bill came back up for a final vote on the House floor.

"Was it a warm and fuzzy conversation? No," Israel recalled. "But that's what a good leader does. I didn't leave that meeting with any doubts as to where she stood."[40] In the end Israel—who described the climate surrounding the final floor vote as feeling like "as much pressure per square inch as has ever been in the House of Representatives"—stood with his party and opposed the GOP-crafted bill.

But his colleague David Wu (D-Ore.) faced a tougher problem. Wu had reservations about the bill but backed it because he saw it as taking care of the nation's sickest and poorest citizens. "The stars align once every twenty-five years, or fewer," he explained. "You take

39. Helen Dewar, "Democrats Push GOP for Greater Inclusion; Bigger Role Sought in Crafting Legislation," *The Washington Post*, Oct. 19, 2003.

40. Israel interview.

the deal and then when you have an opportunity, you fix the problems with legislation."[41] Wu hated the idea of defying Pelosi and other Democratic leaders and told the minority leader he would neither vote early nor issue a press release before the vote endorsing the GOP plan.

As the minutes dragged on, Wu became, in the words of one Democratic lawmaker who asked not to be identified, "catatonic." He refused to vote at all as the vote sat stuck at 216 to 218 in the Democrats' favor. "I didn't want to supply the vote to put them over the top," Wu later said of Republicans.[42] As Wu's colleagues gathered around him, he kept his eyes fixed on the right hand of Representative Richard "Doc" Hastings (R-Fla.), who held the gavel and was the one lawmaker who could bring the vote to a close. Wu had been "gaveled out" before, and he didn't want the record to indicate he had opted out on one of the most important votes in years.

Mississippi Democrat Gene Taylor, known for his irreverent sense of humor, decided to poke fun at his colleague from the Pacific Northwest. Taylor went over to Representative Patrick Kennedy (D-R.I.), John F. Kennedy's nephew, who was sleeping on a couch in the Democratic cloakroom. He kicked Kennedy in the foot to wake him up, and got the congressman to invoke his late uncle by declaring on the House floor, "Ask not what your country can do for Wu, but what Wu can do for your country!"[43] Wu, focused on the podium, did not respond even as his colleagues roared at the joke.

As the Republicans desperately sought out needed votes—then-Health and Human Services Secretary Tommy G. Thompson flouted Capitol Hill convention and worked over members on the House floor—some lawmakers took refuge elsewhere. Boehner and his friend Latham went out to the balcony off the Speaker's Lobby, rolled themselves up in their coats, and went to sleep, only to wake up at the

41. David Wu, interview with author, July 12, 2005.

42. Ibid.

43. Gene Taylor, interview with author, July 28, 2005.

sound of the final roll call bells. Peterson brushed off Pelosi, who was making a last-minute attempt to get his vote, and went to the GOP cloakroom. Finally, two conservative Republicans, Trent Franks (Arizona) and C. L. "Butch" Otter (Idaho) switched their votes, allowing Wu to vote aye without casting the deciding vote. A few other members switched their votes and the measure passed 220 to 215.

"It was one of the ugliest moments I've ever seen on the House floor," recalled Billy Tauzin, who helped write the bill. "And I've seen some ugly moments."[44]

Hastert made no apologies for the harsh way he and his lieutenants managed to eke out a victory. "They criticize me for keeping the vote open so long," he said in a statement after it passed, "but I've been working that issue for 20 years, and seniors have been waiting through three Congresses for a prescription drug benefit. So I don't think waiting three hours to get it done is too much."

But Gutknecht, one of the Republicans who refused to bend on the bill, said most members "felt that was way over the top." Gutknecht likes to quote former British Prime Minister Margaret Thatcher, who has said that when it comes to public policy, first you win the debate and then you win the vote. "The leadership has said on several occasions we don't have to win the debate, we already have the votes. . . . People are willing to tolerate [that kind of behavior] up to a point. But people are almost up to that point."[45]

Wu devoted months to making amends in the Democratic Caucus and shunned pharmaceutical industry contributions to show his constituents he cast his vote for policy, not financial, reasons. But some of his colleagues still believe he robbed them of an enormous political victory; a year after the vote, Barney Frank told Wu he had underestimated how personally lawmakers take party defections on key votes. A former corporate lawyer, Wu used to think of the House

44. Tauzin interview.

45. Gutknecht interview.

as "a 435-member law firm." But he came to recognize "this is the most personal of politics, and you should keep that in mind."[46]

The Medicare vote was not the only time in recent years House leaders have decided national policy late in the night, well past reporters' daily deadlines. From May to July of 2003, for example, they passed a major tax cut bill at 1:56 a.m., cut Head Start funding in a 12:57 a.m. vote, and approved $87 billion for the war in Iraq at 12:12 a.m. Two years later GOP leaders held open a vote approving the Central American Free Trade Agreement for more than an hour; they passed it just after midnight, with 15 Democratic aye votes, by a margin of 217 to 215. Sherrod Brown argued in an opinion piece that these late-night votes amounted to a "subversion of democracy" because the public cannot observe the legislative wrangling that produces these narrow victories.

"You can do a lot in the middle of the night, under the cover of darkness," he wrote.[47]

Within a single week in November 2004, this majority-focused strategy of governing reached a crescendo. On Wednesday, November 17, the GOP Conference voted to ensure that if state prosecutors managed to indict Tom DeLay, he would be able to remain the chamber's second-ranking leader. In doing so Republicans reversed the rule they had adopted in 1993 to show voters they were ethically purer than the entrenched Democratic majority, which had protected then-Ways and Means Committee Chairman (and later convicted felon) Dan Rostenkowski. The decision took place behind closed doors. When a couple of members suggested they take a recorded vote on the matter, other Republicans drowned them out with a chorus of "Nos."

46. Wu interview.

47. Sherrod Brown, "Under the Cover of Darkness," *St. Louis Post Dispatch*, Dec. 11, 2003.

Then on Saturday the twentieth, Republicans again huddled privately to decide if they should bring up a bill reorganizing the nation's intelligence community for a floor vote. The measure—reflecting the work of a national bipartisan commission that spent years studying how intelligence failures contributed to the September 11 terrorist attacks on New York and Washington—had the backing of President Bush, Speaker Hastert, and most House Democrats. It was headed to easy passage. Hastert, however, was worried about GOP opposition to the bill, since some conservatives believed it might unduly undermine the Pentagon's authority and that it lacked sufficient measures to crack down on illegal immigration. Hastert abruptly decided to pull the bill, on the grounds that his job is to please "a majority of the majority."[48] (See the full text of Hastert's speech on pages 153–57.)

Critics saw both moves as an indication of Republicans' willingness to allow their members' interests to trump the needs and desires of Americans who might be concerned about national security or about the ethical standards of their elected representatives. To Hastert and his top deputies these were minor worries: they had just made history a few weeks before by expanding their majority for the second time in a row, something Republicans hadn't done in the past century. After spending several elections struggling to hold onto control of the House, Republicans were now firmly in charge.

A few outspoken Republicans, however, questioned the wisdom of this strategy. Zach Wamp, a Tennessee firebrand who came in with the Class of 1994, called the DeLay rules change "a PR disaster. There's no way to explain it." The leadership, he said, "is on a roll, and as a result we as a conference made a mistake today about the future."[49] After several House Republicans complained and DeLay assured his colleagues he would not be indicted, the Conference reversed the rules change in January 2005. Delay may have regretted

48. Charles Babington, "Hastert Launches a Partisan Policy," *The Washington Post*, Nov. 27, 2004.

49. Zach Wamp, interview with author, Nov. 17, 2004.

that decision nine months later, when a Travis County grand jury indicted him and he had no choice but to relinquish his leadership post.

Some rank-and-file members felt a similar sense of unease about Hastert's decision to pull the intelligence bill, which had broad support among Democrats (and eventually passed the House December 7 by a margin of 336 to 75, with only 67 Republicans in opposition). The families of victims of the September 11, 2001, terrorist attacks issued a statement saying it was "particularly troubling" that Hastert failed to bring the intelligence bill up for a vote since it was clear it would have passed by a broad majority.[50]

While the Republican leaders ultimately backed away from the precipice by jettisoning the DeLay rules change and allowing the intelligence bill to come to a vote, neither incident has prompted them to reassess the way they run the House. Dan Mattoon, an influential Washington lobbyist and one of Hastert's closest friends, described Hastert in an interview as "probably the strongest speaker in modern times, in terms of his ability to manage the House." Hastert's affable demeanor makes his governing style look gentler than it actually is, Mattoon added: "It doesn't look like he's strong-arming you until it's over and you've gone home."[51]

Nancy Pelosi, who boasts a ready smile and frequently dispenses high-quality chocolate to her colleagues, has proven herself as adept in twisting arms as Hastert. In countless closed-door meetings, she has suggested that any Democrat who breaks ranks on a high-profile vote is undercutting the party's chances of regaining the majority. She invoked this scenario at least three weeks in a row in Democratic Caucus meetings leading up to the July 2005 vote on the Central

50. Babington, "Hastert Launches a Partisan Policy."
51. Dan Mattoon, interview with author, Mar. 11, 2005.

American Free Trade Agreement, according to Representative James P. Moran (D-Va.).

"She said a vote for CAFTA is a vote to let a Republican off the hook," recalled Moran, who supported the free trade agreement. "It exerted an enormous amount of pressure. All of us felt it."[52]

Centrists such as Moran had more leverage when Bill Clinton was in office, because they could make common cause on issues like trade and welfare reform with the president. But with a Republican in the White House, they are on their own.

The fifteen Democrats who voted in favor of the trade pact quickly began to feel the consequences, from outside interest groups as well as party leaders. A couple of weeks after the vote, Moran spoke at a local AFL-CIO meeting in northern Virginia: nearly half the audience got up and walked out. Union leaders have suggested running primary opponents against New York Democratic Representatives Gregory Meeks and Edolphus Towns in 2006. And Pelosi has made it clear she will remember who crossed party lines.

Moran, who said he admires Pelosi's strength, said she "has an iron will. Sometimes she has to take strong positions that tend to marginalize people who don't agree with her. . . . I'm pleased with Nancy's leadership, but it's tough."[53]

52. James P. Moran, interview with author, Sept. 1, 2005.
53. Ibid.

CHAPTER 4

House Centrists Disappear

The debate has become more stifled out of the fear that members have that it will cost them. . . . We're losing touch with what ordinary Americans are thinking.

—Connecticut Representative
Christopher Shays,
a moderate Republican

When the Caucus goes one way and you go another, you're isolated for a while. This can be a very lonely place.

—Representative David Wu (D-Ore.),
who crossed party lines on
the 2003 Medicare vote

Four days after the 2004 election, Democratic Representative Collin Peterson's phone rang in Minnesota. It was John P. "Jack" Murtha, the crusty but affectionate Pennsylvania Democrat known for playing inside-the-Beltway politics better than almost anyone.

"There's a bunch of goddamned people maneuvering around," Murtha told the eight-term House veteran who was vying for his party's top spot on the Agriculture Committee. "You've got to pay your goddamn dues."[1]

Murtha—who swears frequently as long as women are not within earshot—was referring to the money that senior Democrats must give

Epigraphs. Christopher Shays, interview with author, Nov. 17, 2005; Wu interview.

1. Peterson interview.

each election to the Democratic Congressional Campaign Committee. As a senior Democrat, Peterson owed the committee $45,000 for the 2004 election cycle.

The Minnesota congressman, who had reluctantly donated $25,000 to the DCCC just before the election, did not want to give another penny. His war chest was smaller than most because he didn't engage in the kind of constant fund-raising drive his colleagues did. Moreover Peterson had resented the committee ever since his first congressional bid in 1986, when Democratic campaign officials encouraged him to demand a recount and then abandoned him with $250,000 in legal bills after state officials ruled in favor of his opponent.

But Murtha was adamant. "I don't care," he told Peterson. "Just pay your dues and we'll take care of it."[2]

The tale of how Collin Peterson nearly lost his ranking membership bid on the Agriculture Committee in 2005 speaks more to the status of centrists in the House than almost any other incident in recent years. Peterson's current predicament, as a member with broad popular support back home but little backing in his own party, explains why Democrats and Republicans have encountered such difficulty in reaching consensus on Capitol Hill. Most Democrats see Peterson as a conservative outlier who can't be trusted, while Republicans only reach out to him when they desperately need his vote.

The difficulty that conservative Democrats and moderate Republicans now face in the House—under increasing pressure to fall into line, unable to operate as independent voting blocs—has undermined centrists' influence in the House. They are less able to pressure their respective leaders, so they cannot broker deals between the parties like they did in the past. Legislating on Capitol Hill has suffered as a result.

2. Ibid.

Peterson seems like the quintessential American pol, with his hearty laugh and weathered good looks. He remains one of the few lawmakers who still smokes cigars in the Speaker's Lobby just off the House floor, often while reclining in one of the lobby's high-backed leather chairs. But while Peterson has developed some close friendships during his Capitol Hill tenure, many of his Democratic colleagues view him with suspicion. He ranks as one of the most conservative members in his Caucus. When it comes to his constituents, he explained, "In my district if you're not pro-gun and pro-life and pro-snowmobile, you can't talk to them."[3]

As a result, Peterson often crosses party lines. During the 2004 fight over President Bush's Medicare prescription drug bill, Peterson not only voted for the bill, but he worked with House Ways and Means Committee Chairman Thomas to draft it. (Peterson, along with a few other Democrats from farm states, wanted to ensure that their constituents got a more generous rural health care benefit under Medicare.) At one point during the three-hour vote, the pressure became so intense that Peterson hid out in the Republican cloakroom, where he overheard President Bush trying to round up GOP support through a series of last-minute phone calls.

None of this endeared him to Democratic leaders who have strived mightily in recent years to instill greater party discipline. Peterson is close to Nancy Pelosi—he was an early backer of hers when she ran for whip in 2002—but other top Democrats resent that he provides neither financial nor political support to many of their causes.

So when Representative Charlie Stenholm (D-Tex.) lost his reelection bid in 2004—one of several Texas Democrats felled by Republicans' 2003 redistricting plan—House Democrats had a choice. Should they reward Peterson with their top post on the Agri-

3. Ibid.

culture Committee because he was next in line for the job, or should they make an example of him?

The Democratic Caucus and the Capitol Hill press corps buzzed for weeks with speculation. Peterson made some overtures to the party, paying the balance of his campaign dues. But he still had to appear before the Democratic Steering and Policy Committee for a formal interview before obtaining the position.

Most of the ranking members' interviews take five minutes. Peterson's lasted for more than an hour. Steny Hoyer and George Miller, who at the time served as House minority whip and ranking member on the House Education and Workforce Committee, respectively, grilled him on why he had defected from his party on key votes, since that meant they had to pressure a more vulnerable Democrat to stick with the party in his place.

Peterson, who has won comfortably in his district for years despite its Republican leanings (Bush won it by 56 percent in 2004, 59 percent in 2000), was not amused.

"Let me get this straight," he told his Democratic elders. "I gave you my money, and now you're telling me I should vote against my conscience and vote against my constituents so I can become a marginal member and you can spend two million bucks to save my ass? You guys have to understand you're not in the majority. You ought to be thankful there are guys like me in the caucus and if you didn't have guys like me you're going to be in the minority for a long time."[4]

The room fell silent. Steering committee members approved Peterson's bid for a promotion later that day.

Peterson was not the only centrist Democrat to face a grilling from Caucus leaders. Representative Allen Boyd (D-Fla.) has supported the concept of private Social Security accounts for years, putting him at odds with party officials who had made a priority of killing President Bush's Social Security privatization plan. When Boyd

4. Ibid.

became the lead Democratic co-sponsor of the House GOP's Social Security bill, some lawmakers questioned whether he deserved to retain his spot on the coveted House Appropriations Committee. As Representative Xavier Becerra (California) put it, when it comes to sitting on an exclusive committee, "Those are privileges, not rights. You have to act a leader."[5] House Democrats debated at length whether they should toss Boyd off the powerful spending panel. In the end they decided to let him stay.

Boyd, for his part, believes senior Democrats' drive for total party unity is shortsighted. House Democrats share common goals when it comes to education and the broad role of the federal government, he said, but leaders need to recognize he represents a conservative district. "My loyalty is to the people I represent back home, and not to anyone else," Boyd said, noting that John Kerry got only 42 percent of the vote in his district during the last presidential election. "How do you say to a person like that, 'We the party leaders are going to tell you how to cast your vote on certain issues.' You're basically going to give the seat away."[6]

On a certain level House Democratic leaders realize this—in the end, they chose not to punish Boyd and Peterson. But they only gave these men prized spots in the party hierarchy after humiliating them publicly, and they used Boyd and Peterson to send a message to other like-minded centrists. As the moderates in the chamber have dwindled in number, they have found it harder to make their case. Both parties are seeking to create more cohesive voting blocs, and this leaves little room for iconoclasts.

In at least one instance, Democrats tried to defeat one of their own through the primary process. Representative Cal Dooley (D-Calif.), who served in Congress for fourteen years before retiring in 2004, earned a reputation in Washington as an independent centrist who was willing to buck his leadership on free trade and other fiscal

5. Xavier Becerra, interview with author, Mar. 7, 2005.
6. Allen Boyd, interview with author, Mar. 10, 2005.

issues. Dooley tried repeatedly to land a seat on the exclusive Appropriations Committee but gave up trying when he concluded his party's leaders were intent on denying him the plum slot. But the leadership took it a step further when then-California state Senator Jim Costa came to town along with other state Democratic officials a few years ago. Two senior Democrats took Costa aside and asked if he would be willing to challenge Dooley in the 2000 primary.

"They were frustrated that he was more likely to plot his own course and was not as likely to be a team player as they would like," said Costa, who declined the offer. "I would never do that. Cal and I were friends."[7] In the end all sides got what they wanted: Dooley decided to retire in 2004, and Costa succeeded him.

Several decades ago the two parties were more ideologically diverse. House Democrats had in their ranks more Southern conservatives, who infuriated liberal leaders at times but helped ensure the party's majority for decades. The GOP Conference served as home to a fair number of Northeastern Republicans, who would sometimes make common cause with the Democrats on civil rights legislation and other progressive bills but would remain within the party fold.

"When the Democrats were in control we sought bipartisan deals because we often lost some of our own, especially Southern Dixiecrats," recalled Henry Waxman (D-Calif.).[8] As Waxman's top aide Phil Schiliro put it in the same interview, "I would like to say Democrats did bipartisan things because we were good guys. We did it out of necessity."[9]

But over the course of the past thirty years, the parties sorted themselves out across the political spectrum. Northern Republicans moved to the South and kept voting for the GOP, while many South-

7. Jim Costa, interview with author, Mar. 2, 2005.
8. Waxman interview.
9. Phil Schiliro, interview with author, July 28, 2005.

ern conservatives abandoned their Democratic roots.[10] At the same time Democrats made some inroads into northeastern GOP strongholds.

A study by political scientists John H. Aldrich and David Rhode, using a measurement of ideological leaning developed by University of Houston Professor Keith Poole and Princeton University Professor Howard Rosenthal, demonstrates how these shifts have affected voting patterns in the House. The scale, known as "DW-NOMINATE," ranks lawmakers from the most liberal to the most conservative end of the spectrum. Aldrich and Rhode compared the ideological scores for the 91st Congress, which took office at the start of the Nixon administration, with the 105th Congress, two years after the GOP took control of the House. In the 91st, Congressional Democrats surfaced in all ten of the political scale's groups, while Republicans belonged to all but the most liberal group. By the 105th Congress Republicans were confined to the most conservative half of the spectrum while the four most liberal categories were limited only to Democrats.

"The contrast could not be starker," Aldrich and Rhode wrote. "The separation of each party from the other is almost the maximum possible."[11]

The tale of three men who crossed paths in the summer of 1961 illustrates how Capitol Hill has changed in recent years. John Lewis, a student civil rights leader from Alabama, and Cornell student Bob Filner traveled on the same bus as "Freedom Riders" that year to protest the segregated seating of interstate passengers in the South. They got arrested in Jackson, Mississippi, by the head of the state's National Guard. That Mississippi National Guard leader, G. V.

10. Nelson W. Polsby, *How Congress Evolves: Social Bases of Institutional Change* (Oxford: Oxford University Press, 2004).

11. John H. Aldrich and David W. Rhode, "The Logic of Conditional Party Government: Revisiting the Electoral Connection," in *Congress Revisited*, 7th ed. (Washington, D.C.: CQ Press, 2001), 269–292.

"Sonny" Montgomery, later won a seat in the House of Representatives as a Democrat, as did Filner and Lewis. In the early 1990s all three men served comfortably together as members of the House Democratic Caucus from Mississippi, California, and Georgia, even joking of how they once faced off against each other. But Montgomery retired in 1994 and a conservative southern Republican—Charles "Chip" Pickering—not a conservative Democrat, took his place. The Caucus in which Filner and Lewis continued to serve became more homogeneous, and it lost the kind of ideological diversity that had forced its members in the past to seek the political center.

Even lawmakers who started off seeking a middle ground in Congress have moved more in line with their party in recent years. Two years after taking office in 1999, Ellen Tauscher (D-Calif.) got a 68 percent favorable rating from the U.S. Chamber of Commerce, which placed her in the Democrats' more conservative wing. By 2003 her Chamber rating had dropped to 40 percent. The association's lobbyists attribute this shift to Tauscher's safer congressional district—after the 2000 Census Democrats boosted her seat's Democratic performance by shifting GOP voters into a neighboring district—saying this allowed her to show her more liberal stripes. Tauscher blames the House GOP for putting up legislation she considers too partisan to support. In either case, the shift shows how one of the House's prominent centrists has moved solidly into the Democrats' camp.

Centrists' decline reflects a sort of political "perfect storm"—their districts are disappearing as the two parties push for more lopsided congressional seats, their smaller ranks diminish their political relevance in the House, and party leaders' increasingly harsh tactics leave them little room to maneuver. House moderates today are outnumbered and intimidated.

Northeastern moderate Republicans are a disappearing species. This House group has significantly changed its voting behavior over the past decade, providing critical support to their party's agenda. While House conservatives may grab more headlines, GOP moderates have done just as much to ensure the continuing success of the Republican Revolution.

When the GOP first took power, its centrists were willing to flex their political muscle on occasion. Several prominent Republican moderates had backed Newt Gingrich early on, including Steve Gunderson (Wisconsin) and Nancy Johnson (Connecticut). They would successfully remind Gingrich of this fact when he pursued policies they couldn't abide. When Republican conservatives pushed to roll back longstanding environmental and workers' safety protections, these moderates formed alliances with Democrats and forced the GOP leadership to back down.

Over time, however, GOP moderates lost their nerve. The turning point came during the 1998 drive to impeach President Clinton. Centrists in the House could have derailed the process. Nearly a dozen moderates held occasional conference calls to plot strategy but as one participant said, "By the time you got everyone on the phone the call was about to end, and nobody could figure out what to do."[12] While some of these members would have considered censuring rather than impeaching Clinton, DeLay refused to allow such a vote. That left these members in a bind. They searched for another way out.

Some came up with the idea of writing a letter urging the Senate not to convict Clinton even if the House impeached him. While they intended to release the letter before the final House vote, several lawmakers dropped out at the last minute, so in the end just four Republicans issued the joint statement a couple of days after lawmakers impeached Clinton. Most outsiders wondered why they would pen a letter after the fact, saying while Clinton's actions were "severe enough" to warrant impeachment, "We are not convinced and do not

12. Phone call participant who asked not to be identified, interview with author, Apr. 1, 2005.

want our votes interpreted to mean that we view removal from office as the only reasonable conclusion to this case."[13]

Even conservatives who broke party ranks during the impeachment proceedings suffered politically. Mark Souder is on the far right of the political spectrum, an opponent of abortion, gun control, and taxes. But he concluded that the impeachment managers had failed to prove three of their four counts against Clinton and voted aye on just one charge, obstruction of justice. In the wake of his vote, most of his finance committee quit, saying they couldn't raise money for him. He faced a primary opponent not just in 2000 but also in every election since then, and he lost significant support among self-identified Republican men in the aftermath of the impeachment. In September 2004 a firefighter in Souder's hometown of Grabill approached him at a parade and told him, "I'll never vote for you because of your impeachment vote."[14]

At the time of the impeachment debate, more than two dozen Republicans told Souder they wanted to follow his lead but feared a primary challenge: while national polls indicated roughly 60 percent of Americans opposed impeaching Clinton, this meant nothing in lopsided GOP-held House districts. Several Democrats confided in Souder that they would have backed a single impeachment charge against the president but had worried they would suffer politically in left-leaning districts. "The fact remains nobody broke ranks with their district. When I did break ranks with my district I got piled on, and everybody knew it," Souder said. "The Clinton question, at the end of the day, became not a legal question but a partisan question."[15]

Since the impeachment, divisions between the parties have only deepened. The voting record of Republican moderates highlights how effective party leaders have been in imposing discipline. New York

13. Dan Balz and Helen Dewar, "Byrd Raises Possibility of Avoiding Senate Trial," *The Washington Post*, Dec. 22, 1998.

14. Souder interview.

15. Ibid.

Representative Peter King, who voted against impeaching Clinton, sided with his leaders 91 percent of the time between June 1, 2004, and March 31, 2005. During that same period fellow New Yorker Sherwood Boehlert toed the party line 88 percent of the time, and Christopher Shays voted 85 percent of the time with top Republicans.[16] On average, House Republicans now vote with President Bush slightly more than 90 percent of the time.

There is no room for middle ground anymore, and in some ways this has made Congress less effective. Its members are less likely to assert institutional prerogatives, because they feel more closely tied to their party than to the body in which they serve. This aspect of polarization was less evident in the mid-1990s, when Democrats had the presidency and Republicans ruled Congress, because the two branches fought over control of public policy. Now that the GOP controls both the executive and legislative branches, congressional leaders are loath to start investigations or challenge the president.

"[In] the partisan polarization of American politics, members of Congress tend to view themselves less as members of a separate and equal institution, with its own oath of office and obligations, and more as either a part of the president's team or a part of the opposition to the president," said Mickey Edwards. "What is needed is serious surgery: the Congress needs a backbone."[17]

While the voting behavior of GOP moderates may seem puzzling at times, it makes sense when viewed in a broader political context. First, liberal Republicans are often more wedded to the party than their conservative counterparts. "Unlike the conservatives, the moderates are party loyalists," said David Goldston, who has spent two

16. *Congressional Quarterly* member profiles.

17. Mickey Edwards, "Checks and Balances, Perspectives on American Democracy" (speech, Center for American Progress and American University, St. Regis Hotel, Washington, D.C., Aug. 31, 2005).

decades working for Boehlert.[18] Unlike conservatives who see the GOP as simply a means for achieving their ideological goals, Goldston said, moderates tend to be more attached to the party as an institution.

Second, moderate Republicans live in fear of losing their party's primary. In 2002, for example, Boehlert won his primary contest with Cayuga County legislator David L. Walrath by just three thousand votes. Walrath challenged him again two years later. After that first primary scare, Boehlert adopted a series of more conservative positions, voting for a ban on what opponents call "partial-birth abortion" and endorsing a House Republican attempt to overturn Washington, D.C.'s gun control laws.

Some Democrats envy that Republicans can impose party discipline so effectively through their primaries. "We can't take Allen Boyd out in a primary because we couldn't elect a Democrat to keep his seat," said Sherrod Brown, a prominent House liberal. "Somehow they can do that, and we haven't."[19]

Third, moderate Republicans have gained seniority over time, and this boosts their incentive to work with party leaders. Boehlert now chairs the House Science Committee, while Fred Upton (Michigan) heads an Energy and Commerce subcommittee and is hoping to take over the full committee's gavel in a few years. Representative James Greenwood (R-Penn.) chaired an Energy and Commerce subcommittee before retiring in 2004, and his voting record became more conservative toward the end of his House tenure. In 2003 he voted with his party 88 percent of the time, compared with 68 percent of the time five years before.[20] "Over a period of time they've become willing to be a part of the team," said Bill Paxon, who chaired the House GOP leadership before retiring from Congress in the late

18. David Goldston, interview with author, Mar. 25, 2005.
19. Brown interview.
20. *Congressional Quarterly* member profiles.

House Speaker Newt Gingrich (R-Ga.) and his wife, Marianne, walk with Rep. Robert Livingston (R-La.) and his wife, Bonnie, and daughter Susie into a GOP leadership election meeting in November 1998. That day Republicans chose Livingston to succeed Gingrich as Speaker, though Livingston gave up the post a month later during the impeachment of President Clinton.

Ray Lustig/The Washington Post

Speaker Gingrich walks with Rep. Steve Horn (R-Calif.) during a pause in Clinton's impeachment proceedings in December 1998. Horn later became the only California incumbent to lose his seat in 2002 as a result of redistricting.

Ray Lustig/The Washington Post

House minority leader Richard A. Gephardt (D-Mo.) realized that the controversy over appointing a new House chaplain damaged his relationship with Speaker J. Dennis Hastert (R-Ill.) but also thought that Hastert botched a real effort to achieve bipartisanship. "It was maddening, it was frustrating," Gephardt said.
Bill O'Leary/The Washington Post

Minority leader Gephardt and Rep. Patrick Kennedy (D-R.I.) make fund-raising calls for the 2000 elections at Democratic headquarters. Gephardt raised record sums for his party in an unsuccessful effort to retake the House.
Bill O'Leary/The Washington Post

House majority leader Richard K. Armey (R-Tex.) takes notes during President Clinton's last State of the Union speech in January 2000.
Robert A. Reeder/The Washington Post

Speaker Hastert (middle) and Majority Leader Armey (right), sitting with Senate majority leader Trent Lott (left), meet after holding a press conference to complain of President Clinton's approach to budget negotiations in September 2000.

Ray Lustig/The Washington Post

Minority leader Gephardt congratulates Nancy Pelosi in October 2001 on becoming House minority whip; Pelosi later succeeded Gephardt after his retirement from office.

Ray Lustig/The Washington Post

House majority whip Tom DeLay (R-Tex.) (right) passes a velvet hammer to House majority whip Roy Blunt (R-Mo.) (left) in November 2002 as Speaker Hastert looks on; DeLay's tough tactics with lobbyists as well as lawmakers earned him the nickname "The Hammer" as he rose to power.

Frank Johnston/The Washington Post

Speaker Hastert and Minority Leader Pelosi greet colleagues and visitors during the opening ceremonies of the 108th Congress in January 2003. The two leaders rarely have face-to-face meetings.

Bill O'Leary/The Washington Post

1990s. "They're moving up to chair committees and subcommittees."[21]

Fourth, and perhaps most important, Republican moderates pay a price when they stray from the fold. The examples are endless: Shays, whose successful campaign to enact campaign finance legislation over House leaders' objections cost him the chairmanship of the House Government Reform Committee; Bass, who lost his position as deputy whip after defying the leadership on a single vote; and Leach, who failed to get the helm of the House International Relations Committee after questioning Gingrich's ethics and refusing to engage in the kind of fund-raising frenzy his party demanded. "If, like me, you ignore the rules you can expect consequences," Leach said.[22]

Even lawmakers who generally get along with House leaders can run into trouble if they contradict senior Republicans on a politically charged issue. Heather Wilson is more of a conservative than a moderate, but she is one of the few House members who represents a competitive district. As such she pays keen attention to what her constituents think. When she challenged Energy and Commerce Committee Chairman Joe Barton (R-Tex.) on a single amendment during a debate over the president's Medicare bill, he punished her by forcing her to relinquish a spot on the House Armed Services Committee. "People in fewer and fewer districts have to listen to more" mainstream voters, Wilson said. "For most of my colleagues, getting elected is a formality."[23]

Leaders from both parties have asserted their influence through both institutional changes and ad hoc maneuvers in recent years. House Republicans' decision to impose six-year term limits on committee chairs has enhanced the leadership's influence exponentially,

21. Paxon interview.
22. James Leach, interview with author, Feb. 10, 2005.
23. Wilson interview.

since it prevents other senior-ranking Republicans from establishing an independent power base. (It's worth noting that GOP leaders have made only one exception to this rule. Hastert decided David Dreier could remain Rules Committee chair during the 109th Congress because the panel amounted to an arm of the leadership.) By his or her fifth year a committee chair is already a lame duck, watching more junior members lobbying for the top spot. In this climate it's hard for the chair to intimidate fellow members or to rally support from the outside lobbying community, who could help counter pressure from the leadership.

Until recently, House Democrats continued to operate under a system where ranking members—the leader of the minority party on a committee—maintained an unusual amount of sway over the Caucus. Bob Filner, who taught history for two decades at San Diego State University, described the House as "a feudal institution. The only way you can get anything done around here is through personal relationships, lord-vassal relationships. . . . You kiss the ring, or kiss the rear end of your chairman. If they don't like you you're finished. It's not about issues."[24]

Filner has been both the beneficiary and the victim of this feudal system. At one point early in his career, he challenged his ranking member, then-Representative Norm Mineta (D-Calif.), on a transportation matter. Mineta made his life miserable as a result. Another time he defied John Dingell, even daring to call him by his first name in a private meeting of House Democrats. Dingell didn't speak to him for the next eight years.

But Filner once buckled under pressure and withdrew a proposed rule change that would have curtailed the power of committee chairs, and Richard Gephardt made sure Filner's district got several hundred million dollars in federal funds for a sewage treatment plant as compensation. (Filner touts the Tijuana River Valley plant on his website

24. Filner interview.

as part of his personal biography.) A few years later Filner raised $500,000 at a single fund-raising event for House Democrats in San Diego. Gephardt rewarded him by inviting him to a secretive leadership meeting.

"There's always another room of a smaller group that they tell you about when they want to reward you. . . . The rank and file do not have a lot to say about things," Filner said. "Everybody thought they'd be back in power the next time and the next time, so nobody changed their behavior."[25]

With powerful leaders on both sides reinforcing divisions between the parties, members have a hard time finding common ground. Filner described the following difficulty: one of his constituents, a dentist, complained about an Occupational Safety and Health Administration (OSHA) rule mandating he maintain a shower on site because he keeps a dangerous chemical in a small vial that he uses in one or two operations a year. Determined to fix this "stupid rule," Filner went to Democratic leaders and suggested they change it.

"The Democrats said, 'You can't do that.'" Filner said. "I said, 'What do you mean, I can't?' They said, 'People will say you're trying to undermine OSHA.'"

So he went to the Republicans and they told him, "If you do that, we could use that as a vehicle to undermine OSHA."

Filner was stuck, and abandoned his plan to change the rule. "Your own constituents don't understand at all why these common things can't get passed," he said, but it's impossible when both parties are trying to game the system "rather than just solving the problem."[26]

Academics are still debating whether Americans are drifting apart politically or whether it is just the elites who are becoming more distant. In his recent book *Culture War? The Myth of a Polarized*

25. Ibid.
26. Ibid.

America, Stanford University Professor Morris P. Fiorina suggests Democratic and Republican voters share more in terms of ideology than some would think. Similar numbers of "blue state" and "red state" residents believe the government is "almost always" wasteful and inefficient. The two groups are just as likely to think big corporations have too much power and make too much money.[27] A solid majority of these voters "see themselves as positioned between two relatively extreme parties,"[28] but since both parties are moving apart at a similar rate, these Americans are stuck. "Voters will be less enthusiastic about their choices and about election outcomes than previously, but given a choice between two extremes, they can only elect an extremist," he writes.[29]

In the meantime centrist lawmakers in both parties are becoming discouraged. Dooley decided to retire in 2004 partly because he was tired of playing such a small role in shaping national policy. "A lot of what members are struggling with is how do you maintain a sense of self-worth when you're coming back to Washington to vote on naming a post office or voting on a suspension bill," said Dooley, who now heads the National Food Processors Association. "I got bored."[30]

Even lobbyists have adjusted their work accordingly, focusing their efforts on a dwindling number of House members. Bill Miller, vice president and political director for the U.S. Chamber of Commerce, said his list of persuadable lawmakers has dropped by two-thirds over the past several years. "Our target list in the House on any issue is never more than 40," he said. "Out of 435 [representatives], that's bad."[31]

Another business lobbyist, who asked not to be identified, said

27. Morris P. Fiorina, with Samuel J. Abrams and Jeremy C. Pope, *Culture War? The Myth of a Polarized America* (New York: Pearson-Longman, 2005), 11–12.

28. Ibid, 17–19.

29. Ibid, 80.

30. Cal Dooley, interview with author, Feb. 9, 2005.

31. Bill Miller, interview with author, Feb. 23, 2005.

he now spends at least 70 percent of his time focused on the Senate because the House votes in favor of corporate interests so predictably. "I used to spend a lot of time in the House," the lobbyist said. "Why would I spend time in the House now? It just does everything we want."[32]

Some academics point out that the Senate has become more polarized over the past decade as well, and none of this change can be attributed to redistricting. But this ignores the fact that more House ideologues have been winning Senate seats in recent years, such as Rick Santorum (Pennsylvania), Tom Coburn (Oklahoma), and David Vitter (Louisiana) on the Republican side and Charles Schumer (New York) and Barbara Boxer (California) on the Democratic side.

In such a small chamber, the influx of a few committed partisans can make an enormous difference. Many of these conservatives and liberals came from the House—the number of former House members now serving in the Senate has reached an all-time high of fifty-two—and they brought polarization along with them to the upper chamber.[33]

Senator Sam Brownback (R-Kans.), who came to the House with the Class of 1994 but quickly moved to fill the place of Senate Majority Leader Robert Dole (R-Kans.) when Dole ran for president, sees himself as much more conservative.

"It's more ideological in the Senate," Brownback said, adding he thinks his and other partisans' success reflects the fact that the public has become more polarized. A decade ago, "People just said there are two ways to look at the world, you can look at the world from the

32. Business lobbyist who asked not to be identified, interview with author, Feb. 24, 2005.

33. Senate Historian Office. By contrast, the historical average of former House members in the Senate is thirty-eight. In 1995, when Republicans won control of Congress, forty former House members held Senate seats.

left or you can look at the world from the right. People have decided who they are."[34]

The remaining moderates in the House find themselves in a bind. Shays, a cheery lawmaker who often slings his arm around colleagues' shoulders as he consults with them, seems impervious to public criticism because he's spent so long defying the GOP establishment. But he almost lost his seat last election and now sounds tired at times: "It is not easy being a moderate in the Republican Party."[35]

34. Sam Brownback, interview with author, Mar. 11, 2005.
35. Shays interview.

CHAPTER 5

Reshaping America's Political Map

We saw our opportunities and we took them. Is this the way it ought to work? Of course not.

—Virginia Representative Thomas M. Davis III, who oversaw the House Republicans' 2000 redistricting efforts as chairman of the National Republican Congressional Committee

Both parties are equally bad in regards to wanting to keep power.

—Texas state Senator Jeff Wentworth (R), who chaired his chamber's redistricting committee in 2001

The sprawling grounds of Blackhawk Country Club, nestled among the hills of California's San Ramon Valley, epitomize how the East Bay's nouveaux riches with taste live. Visitors who make it past the guarded gates find themselves looking at an eclectic mix of architecture, from club founder Kenneth Behring's Frank Lloyd Wright–inspired mansion to more Mediterranean-style homes boasting terra cotta roofs and gurgling fountains. Many of the homes, which range in value from $1 million to $32 million, have huge windows; all feature expansive, manicured lawns. The 4,800-acre property sports eleven tennis courts, two basketball courts, and two golf courses, along with such features as a golf newsletter that alerts members with

Epigraphs. Davis interview; Jeff Wentworth, interview with author, June 16, 2005.

helpful updates: "Heavy and continuous rain, coupled with high winds, has rendered playability an option that only the most hearty golfers would attempt."[1]

Until 2003 Representative Ellen Tauscher owned a golf membership at Blackhawk, and the people who lived there were her constituents. (Blackhawk has 1,991 homes, and more than half of these homeowners belong to the club; the rest of the memberships are held by nearby residents who live outside its gates, like Tauscher.) Blackhawk homeowners are businessmen and women who have made it, whether as venture capitalists, biotech entrepreneurs, or successful professionals in other fields. They are overwhelmingly Republican. As a voting bloc they did not support Tauscher in either her first 1996 congressional campaign or subsequent reelections.

Because of those political leanings, when Democratic consultant Michael Berman was drawing new House districts in 2001 to reflect the findings of the most recent U.S. Census, he decided to pluck Blackhawk out of Tauscher's district and give it to her Republican neighbor, Representative Richard Pombo. To compensate, he shifted downtown Stockton, a gritty East Bay city, to a district represented at the time by Democratic Representative Gary Condit. (Another Central Valley Democrat, Dennis Cardoza, replaced Condit in 2002 after Condit—who acknowledged having an affair with murdered D.C. intern Chandra Levy—retired from office.)

The U.S. Constitution calls upon the country to conduct a population count once a decade, and this census serves as the basis of the country's redistricting efforts. The House's membership has stayed constant at 435 since the 63rd Congress in 1913, but legislators must reapportion congressional seats every ten years based on shifting population patterns. Much of the West is expanding rapidly, for example, while some Midwestern and Northeastern states are growing more slowly. After the 2000 Census, state officials set to

1. Blackhawk Country Club, *Greens Department News*, January 2005.

work on redrawing their congressional maps; while federal lawmakers don't sit on the panels or committees that determine House delegations, they often lobby fiercely to influence the shape of their new districts.

Tauscher, a former stockbroker and centrist Democrat who managed to unseat a Republican incumbent, takes pride in her ability to attract crossover voters. She has an impressive collection of colorful power suits, talks about what she's learned from her time working on Wall Street, and fights to defend local economic engines such as the Lawrence Livermore National Laboratory. Over the years many of her constituents have become attached to her, and some protested when Democratic leaders began pulling the district apart. One group of East Bay residents even held a protest reminiscent of the Boston Tea Party, dumping bags of tea in a local fountain to demonstrate their desire to remain in Tauscher's district.

Berman, however, had an agenda of his own. The brother of veteran Representative Howard Berman (D-Calif.), the Democratic consultant has devoted years to shaping a political landscape that favors his party. In 2001, as Berman worked, state Democrats had everything they needed to draw a map to their liking, including control of the governor's mansion and the state legislature. The party had two options: maximize the number of Democratic seats in the state's fifty-three member delegation and risk a GOP-sponsored referendum aimed at overturning the map, or strike a deal with the state's Republican incumbents. Berman and his clients decided to strike a deal.

Working with David Dreier and other California GOP lawmakers, Berman crafted a complex map that protected every single incumbent except for Steve Horn, a moderate Republican occupying a swing seat in the southern part of the state. Members were able to shift unfriendly voters to nearby districts—Representative Lois Capps (D) gave Republicans to her neighbor Elton Gallegly (R) while he delivered some of his more liberal constituents to her. In doing so, both marginal members became untouchable.

Technological advances account for this sophisticated constituent shuffling. Back when California Democrat Phillip Burton redid the state's congressional map in the 1980s—an egregious partisan gerrymander, which badly damaged the California GOP—he estimated a neighborhood's partisan leanings by the kind of cars on the street. (Saabs and Volvos meant wealthy Democrats were living on the block, Buicks indicated middle-class Republicans, and Chevys pointed to middle-class Democratic homes.)[2] Now mapmakers can get detailed information about an area's political makeup—down to the voting history of an individual block—and plug it into a computer, allowing them to carve up neighborhoods with precision. The new software ensures both parties can maximize their partisan advantage in a congressional district, provided they have enough political clout to shepherd a map into law.

The results of California's redistricting couldn't be starker. Not a single incumbent lost his or her election bid after the new map went into effect. Tauscher didn't even have a general election opponent in 2002. In 2004 the state offered just one competitive race—to fill the seat of retiring Democratic Representative Cal Dooley, a Central Valley moderate. The Republicans outspent the Democrats by nearly four to one in the race, but state Senator Jim Costa (D) still won handily, 54 to 46 percent. That same year not a single one of California's 153 federal or state legislative seats listed on the ballot changed party control.

The way California power brokers—as well as veteran politicians in Michigan, Pennsylvania, and elsewhere—reshaped the country's legislative map this decade helps explain why Congress is so split today. Working to protect incumbents across the country, the men and women who drew the nation's current congressional districts made the House less accountable to the public and more divided as

2. John Jacobs, *A Rage for Justice: The Passion and Politics of Phillip Burton* (Berkeley: University of California Press, 1995), 431.

a body. Voters served as unwitting allies in this process, by moving into communities that favor one party over another. This sort of self-segregation makes these politicians' task even easier.

Both Republicans and Democrats share the blame for this phenomenon, although the GOP managed to extract greater political gain in this most recent round of redistricting and nearly ensured its congressional majority for the rest of the decade. While political gerrymandering is nothing new in the United States—Democrats used identical tactics when they had the opportunity in years past—the system has now spiraled out of control, with party operatives engaging in a never-ending game of tit for tat that has alienated voters as well as some of their elected representatives.

California's bipartisan gerrymander represented an unqualified success for the state's incumbents. But some state residents questioned the process from the outset. Latinos protested that the map diluted their voting power because Berman, determined to aid his brother, shifted many of the Hispanics who lived in his brother's Los Angeles-based district to the seat of neighboring Democratic Representative Brad Sherman. This legerdemain prompted a legal challenge by the Mexican-American Legal Defense and Education Fund, which failed. Berman's district remains safely Democratic: about 70 percent of its residents backed Al Gore in the 2000 election.[3]

"It doesn't let communities of interest, whether it's Latinos or cities, fully exercise the influence they could have in any election simply because [the districts] don't conform to those communities of interest," said Xavier Becerra. "People just didn't understand why the changes were being made."[4]

3. John Harwood, "No Contests: House Incumbents Tap Census, Software to Get a Lock on Seats—Latest Redistricting Succeeds in Entrenching Status Quo; More Gridlock Guaranteed—'A Sweetheart Gerrymander,'" *Wall Street Journal*, June 19, 2002.

4. Becerra interview.

Voting Rights Act requirements aimed at ensuring minority voting strength statewide have complicated Democrats' national redistricting strategy, since the law often means voters of color—most of whom are Democrats—end up concentrated in the same district, draining potential support for Democrats elsewhere. This became visible after the 1990 census, when new maps helped a raft of African American and Latino Democrats win House seats but allowed Republicans to make inroads into traditionally Democratic-leaning conservative areas in the South. These majority-minority seats often had minority voting populations hovering around 60 percent, which meant neighboring House districts became disproportionately white.[5]

As a result, the action in most California races has shifted to the primary, where some lawmakers now find themselves being squeezed by ambitious Latino state representatives who are term limited and therefore are constantly eyeing potential opportunities to move up the political food chain. State Representative Juan Vargas (D) is hoping to take out Democratic Representative Bob Filner, a former civil rights activist and professor whose San Diego district has been dominated by minorities for years. Before the redistricting in 2000, 45 percent of Filner's constituents were Latino; Vargas wanted to boost this number to 65 percent. (The bulk of his remaining constituents are African American and Asian, with a small minority of Anglos.) Vargas successfully lobbied other Democrats to extend the district out from the city to the neighboring Imperial Valley, home to many Latino farm workers. Filner's new district is now 55 percent Latino,

5. Section 5 of the Voting Rights Act requires that states with sizeable minority populations, when drawing congressional districts, not diminish minority voting strength statewide. The act, however, does not mandate the creation of "safe" minority districts.

To increase a minority's electoral success, a state could choose to create a greater number of districts in which it is likely, though not quite as likely as in "safe" districts, for minority voters to elect candidates of their choice or candidates who would be willing to take the minority's interests into account. In all cases the overriding standard is that the minority's statewide strength not be diminished by the new plan. See *Georgia v. Ashcroft*, 539 U.S. 461 (2003).

and Vargas plans to challenge the congressman in the 2006 Democratic primary.

"It's the Imperial Valley and here I am, an urban intellectual liberal Democratic Jew, all five of which nobody had ever seen before," Filner said, adding that he now faces a district dominated by agriculture when "I couldn't tell an asparagus from an onion." Filner is fighting to keep his seat: he has learned Spanish and constantly tours his sprawling new district. "I really like the area and the people, and they like me," he added.[6]

Tauscher conducted her own lobbying campaign to preserve some of her district's old remnants, which at one point entailed her arguing with the chain-smoking Berman in his Washington, D.C., hotel room. (The congresswoman and her top aide made their case sitting on the bed in Berman's temporary digs, as the consultant puffed out the window.) Pointing out that she had made inroads with some of Blackhawk's residents, Tauscher pleaded to keep much of her district intact. "Why excise these people just because they have an R after their name?" she asked.[7]

In the end Berman conceded on other points, allowing Tauscher to keep her constituents in an area called Lamarinda (home of the tea party protesters). But Blackhawk became Pombo's, and the Democratic-to-Republican ratio in Tauscher's district increased substantially, from a one-point deficit to a 46 to 39 percent advantage. Last election, the congresswoman won her seat with 66 percent of the vote. Tauscher said she is satisfied with her new district and respects Berman's mastery of "what is perhaps one of the most arcane specialties on the planet. He can slice voting performance and demographics like it's beef carpaccio."[8]

Tauscher's neighbor Pombo, on the other hand, was less thrilled with Berman's performance. He felt excluded from the process, re-

6. Filner interview, Feb. 18, 2005.
7. Ellen Tauscher, interview with author, Mar. 10, 2005.
8. Ibid.

calling several years later, "The only question they asked me was, 'Where is your hometown?'" Pombo found out what his new district looked like when a local reporter called him about it and offered to fax him a copy.[9]

While Berman's savvy maneuvering impressed his clients, it earned Democrats a powerful enemy, GOP Governor Arnold Schwarzenegger. Schwarzenegger, who has become increasingly frustrated with how the Democratic-dominated legislature has resisted enacting his policy proposals, suggested in January 2005 that a panel of retired judges draw the state's political map instead of legislators. At the time this book was being written, he was planning to take the issue directly to voters through a November ballot initiative, since the state legislature is balking at the idea. "The current system is rigged to benefit the interests of those in office and not those who put them there," Schwarzenegger said in his State of the State address in 2005. "We must reform it."[10]

Later that year, however, Schwarzenegger's ballot initiative failed by a wide margin, as did another redistricting effort championed by Democrats in Ohio.

Dreier, who helped draw the state's congressional map after the 2000 Census but did not oppose Schwarzenegger's plan, said he and Democrats produced "a reasonable plan" that has enabled three Californians to rise to the top of three exclusive House committees. "For the people, for the voters, it has worked pretty darned well," he said.[11]

But several California lawmakers from both parties—Democrats such as Becerra, Tauscher, and Jim Costa along with Bill Thomas, a senior Republican—say representatives shouldn't be afraid of a fair fight. Costa put it this way: "As a person who's passionate about

9. Richard W. Pombo, interview with author, Oct. 1, 2005.

10. John M. Broder, "Schwarzenegger Proposes Overhaul of Redistricting," *New York Times*, Jan. 6, 2005.

11. Dreier interview.

representative democracy, I believe competitive seats make for balanced public policy."[12]

Thomas, who sparred with Burton over California redistricting in the 1980s, tried unsuccessfully for several years to place a redistricting reform initiative on the state's ballot. In 2004 even minor parties like the Greens and the Libertarians didn't field a candidate against him, let alone the Democrats.

"I had no one," Thomas said. "That's outrageous. . . . You have the creation of districts that are more selected by the candidate than the constituent."[13]

California incumbents may have commanded the art of political mapmaking, but this mastery comes at significant cost.

While California's recent round of redistricting exemplifies a bipartisan gerrymander, Michigan's new legislative landscape shows what happens when a party takes a partisan approach. Michigan remains one of the country's top battleground states, but Republicans controlled the entire process after the 2000 Census and took full advantage of their position. From the very beginning, the only question was how badly the Democrats would suffer.

Both parties have exploited redistricting to serve their interests over the course of Michigan's history. In one particularly charged incident in 1983, the Democrats ushered through a new districting plan for the state legislature in the middle of the night, even though one of the senators casting the decisive vote had just been recalled from office. (The courts later overturned the plan.) It was no surprise that when the Republicans saw their chance to take a congressional delegation tilted nine to seven in favor of Democrats and flip it the other way, they moved quickly.

The GOP governor at the time, John Engler, at first envisioned

12. Costa interview.

13. Thomas interview.

a delegation leaning eight to seven in favor of Republicans, since the state's shrinking population had cost Michigan's delegation a seat. This meant throwing several Democrats into districts with each other. GOP officials and their business community allies debated whether they could stomach imperiling lawmakers like John Dingell, the longest-serving member of the House. "Big John," as he is known, has dominated state politics for half a century, following in his father's footsteps. Republican operatives who gathered in state party headquarters had a moment's hesitation as they plotted strategy but concluded they might as well throw Dingell into a district with his junior Democratic colleague Lynn Rivers. "A number of people at first blanched, and thought 'John Dingell, what an icon,'" recalled Robert LaBrant, the Michigan Chamber of Commerce's senior vice president for political affairs. But then "a number of us decided, 'Screw John Dingell, that arrogant pompous ass.'"[14]

As in other states, Michigan Republican mapmakers used sophisticated software that could spit out dozens of possible plans in rapid succession. In the early 1990s the state GOP's political director, Terry Marquardt, would have to wait as long as three hours for aides to load the proper computer program when he was drawing electoral maps. (He would ask party aides to install it when he was leaving his Olivet, Michigan, home in the morning; it still wouldn't be up and running when he arrived in Plymouth an hour and forty-five minutes later.) By the time Marquardt drafted the state's congressional districts after the 2000 Census, it took him a matter of minutes to run the software.

Ten years of technological development made the process quicker and sharper. In the spring of 2001, Marquardt unfurled his final version of the congressional map in the governor's ceremonial office at the state capitol building and told Engler the plan would elect nine Republicans and six Democrats. He could tell by the expression on

14. Robert LaBrant, interview with author, Mar. 3, 2005.

his face that the governor was surprised: "It was the classic Engler raise of the eyebrows when he likes something."[15]

The Michigan GOP wasted little time in shepherding through the new plan. The state House of Representatives held one hearing on the 167-page bill at 11:00 at night on July 10, 2001, and passed the measure at 2:35 the following morning.[16]

Democrats fought the GOP's map in court, arguing in part that the plan disenfranchised Michigan voters who gave Democrats 52 percent of the vote in the 2000 congressional elections compared with the GOP's 46 percent.[17] Dingell, who headed the legal effort, said, "We knew the deck was stacked but we knew it was the only game in town. We had to play."[18] The Democrats lost. While lawmakers later discovered the Republicans' hasty push for their plan had flaws, including that it failed to assign 4,578 voters to any of the state's fifteen districts, the Republican Secretary of the Senate remedied the situation by drafting a new bill that she sent directly to the governor. Engler signed the bill at 4:54 on the afternoon of September 11, 2001, attracting little attention in the midst of the worst terrorist attack in U.S. history.[19] One of the beneficiaries of the map was Michigan Republican Thaddeus McCotter, who won the following year in a House district he helped craft as chair of the state senate redistricting committee.

The new map put Democratic incumbents like Lynn Rivers in a fix. She found herself under fire from former allies, as groups like the

15. Terry Marquardt, interview with author, Mar. 4, 2005.

16. Sam Hirsch, "The United States House of Unrepresentatives: What Went Wrong in the Latest Round of Congressional Redistricting," *Election Law Journal* 2 (Nov. 2, 2003): 206.

17. George Weeks, "Redrawn Districts Cost Dems; Republican Proposal Would Give State GOP a 9-6 Edge in Congress," *Detroit News*, June 15, 2001.

18. Dingell interview.

19. Hirsch, "The United States House of Unrepresentatives," 207.

United Auto Workers rallied to Dingell's side. "That sort of thing is very hard to take. That sort of thing rocks your world," said Rivers, who lost to Dingell and now teaches in Michigan and hosts a weekly talk show on a local public radio station. "Not only did friendships break apart, long-term political alliances broke apart."[20]

Dingell, with the aid of his wife Debra, launched an aggressive campaign to keep his seat. He mobilized the Washington interests he had cultivated for years, such as the telecommunications and energy industries, touted his lengthy environmental record, and ignored the polling indicating he might lose. The dean of the House had faced tough races in the past, including a 1964 Democratic primary contest against then-Representative John Lesinski Jr., a civil rights opponent. "We knew what we had to do to win elections," he said.[21] Dingell won with 59 percent of the vote.

Other Democratic incumbents saddled with unpalatable districts, James Barcia and Minority Whip David Bonior, chose not to run for reelection in 2002. At the same time previously vulnerable Republicans such as Representative Mike Rogers, who had won his first congressional bid in 2000 by fewer than one hundred votes, cruised to victory.

California's and Michigan's redistricting drives were not the exception; across the country party leaders worked to shore up incumbents by drawing safer districts, producing maps that inoculated both parties from electoral defeat or ensured that one party dominated the political playing field. In Florida, Pennsylvania, and Texas (which underwent a second round of redistricting in 2003), Republicans transformed more-balanced congressional delegations into ones that overwhelmingly favored the GOP. Democrats did the same for their party in Maryland and Georgia. Now that Republicans control Geor-

20. Lynn Rivers, interview with author, Mar. 5, 2005.

21. Dingell interview.

gia's legislature and governorship, however, they have redrawn the map to keep one of the state's competitive seats in GOP hands while potentially threatening a pair of Democratic incumbents. In other states like Illinois and New Jersey, Democrats and Republicans collaborated to shelter their parties' incumbents.

Tom Davis, who chaired the National Republican Congressional Committee from 1998 to 2002, explained his party's strategy to consolidate its hold on the House in an interview. The idea was to "try to solidify what we had, and take the seats out of competition. . . . We'll take care of incumbents. That works to our advantage, since we've got the lead."[22]

Former Representative Martin Frost (D-Tex.), who chaired the House Democrats' campaign arm during the 1996 and 1998 elections and had lobbied his party for years to devote more time and money to redistricting, admitted that the GOP outmaneuvered his party on the issue. "The Republicans were more successful because they were tougher and meaner and more resourceful," said Frost, who lost his seat in 2004 after Texas Republicans shoved him into a solidly Republican district with fellow incumbent Pete Sessions (R).[23]

The November 2002 elections produced the exact results DeLay and his colleagues had anticipated. That year House political analyst Charlie Cook determined that only 11 of the nation's 435 House races ranked as a "toss-up" in which the two parties had an even chance of winning; a decade before Cook had put four times as many seats in that category.[24] Most races weren't even a contest, since 91 percent of incumbents ran unopposed or faced poorly financed opponents.[25] Just four of them lost their seats to challengers that year, a

22. Davis interview.
23. Martin Frost, interview with author, Mar. 11, 2005.
24. *Cook Political Report*, May 28, 2002.
25. Common Cause press office.

new low in modern congressional elections. On average, winning House candidates won a larger percentage of the popular vote than in any House election in more than fifty years.[26] House Republican rule continued.

The recent boost in House incumbents' reelection rate—it has hovered at 98 percent for the past three elections, compared with an average of 93.7 percent in the 1990s[27]—confirms the rigidity of current congressional seats. As Vanderbilt University political scientist Bruce I. Oppenheimer observed, "More congressional districts today are overwhelmingly safe Democratic or safe Republican seats than at any point since 1960, at least."[28]

David Winston, a GOP pollster who has helped his party draw congressional lines for the past three decades, said the aim of any savvy redistricting staffer is to construct seats "resistant to demographic change and political change. The whole goal is to stabilize outcomes."[29]

While Winston is one of the nation's experts when it comes to manipulating maps, he now sees the process as anathema to democracy. National and state political operatives now determine an election's outcome, rather than voters. "You have a political process that disenfranchises everybody," he said. "Congressional elections are now occurring every ten years."[30]

Partisan gerrymandering has a long history in the United States, of course. The name stems from Massachusetts Gov. Elbridge Gerry's maneuver in the early 1800s to craft district lines that favored his Democratic-Republican Party over the Federalists. One of the con-

26. Hirsch, "The United States House of Unrepresentatives," 182.

27. Norman J. Ornstein, Thomas E. Mann, and Michael J. Malbin, *Vital Statistics on Congress* (Washington, D.C.: AEI Press, 1982).

28. Bruce I. Oppenheimer, "Deep Red and Blue Congressional Districts: The Causes and Consequences of Declining Party Competitiveness," *Congress Revisited*, 8th ed. (Washington, D.C.: CQ Press, 2005), 135–157.

29. David Winston, interview with author, June 24, 2005.

30. Ibid.

gressional seats he engineered looked like a salamander, so opponents dubbed the practice "gerrymandering." However, the art of manipulating district lines stems back to the first federal congressional elections in 1788, when famed American revolutionary Patrick Henry used his control over the Virginia legislature to draw seats that put Federalist James Madison at a political disadvantage. Madison, who had to contend with several Anti-Federalist counties south of his home base of Orange County, faced his friend James Monroe in the only congressional race that attracted national press coverage that year. In the end Madison prevailed by 336 votes, by appealing to the region's largely Baptist voters who wanted him to defend their religious freedoms and push for the Bill of Rights in Congress.[31] Some modern-day congressional candidates, however, face even more daunting political obstacles.

From the start of the decade, congressional Republicans knew exactly what was at stake when it came to redistricting. When I asked DeLay during a 2003 press conference why he was devoting so much time and energy to redrawing his home state's congressional districts—the majority leader not only helped draw the plan that ended the careers of five Texas Democrats, he called the Federal Aviation Administration and the Justice Department to help track down fifty-one Texas House members who fled the state in an effort to derail the GOP's new map—he answered without hesitation, "I'm the majority leader, and I want more seats."[32]

Before the most recent Census, the Texas delegation was split seventeen to thirteen in favor of Democrats, a ratio that reflected a

31. Gordon Den Boer, ed., *The Documentary History of the First Federal Elections, 1788–1790*, vol. 11 (Madison: University of Wisconsin Press, 1984), 247–424.

32. Juliet Eilperin, "GOP's New Push on Redistricting; House Seats Are at Stake in Colo., Tex.," *The Washington Post*, May 9, 2003.

1991 Democratic gerrymander. After the 2000 Census the state gained two seats and a court-drawn map awarded those districts to Republicans, producing a seventeen to fifteen ratio. The 2003 Republican-drawn map has produced a delegation tilted twenty-one to eleven in favor of Republicans. (One Texas Democrat, Ralph Hall, switched parties and thereby avoided a tough race.) The number is stunning when you consider that Texas Republicans and Democrats privately agree a fair map would produce eighteen Republican and fourteen Democratic seats. Texas GOP state Senator Jeff Wentworth actually offered a plan with this partisan ratio during the 2003 battle, but his proposal garnered just two votes.

Chet Edwards, the only targeted Texas Democrat left standing after the 2004 election, knows what it's like to be yanked around through redistricting better than nearly any other federal lawmaker. He has run in three different districts for the past three elections; in 2004 alone he had to introduce himself to four hundred thousand new constituents. After Republicans turned his compact central Texas seat into a narrow district that runs from the edges of Fort Worth to the suburbs of Houston with three separate media markets, his campaign spending ballooned from $1.6 million in 2002 to $2.6 million in 2004. Last election a dozen of his Texas Republican congressional colleagues campaigned against him, and one of them, Representative Sam Johnson, compared Edwards to Jane Fonda, although the Democrat earned the title "legislator of the year" from a prominent army association in 2003. Even some of his allies call him "dead man walking" because his district gave George Bush 69 percent of the vote compared with John Kerry's 30 percent.

But Edwards, who has skillfully defended both the military and civil liberties on Capitol Hill since coming to Congress in 1991, has no interest in giving up his seat. During his 2004 campaign he ran ads telling voters he would back Bush when he could and would "respectfully disagree" with the president when he couldn't, and fifty thousand of his constituents pulled the lever for both men in 2004.[33]

Edwards's grueling campaign experience—he narrowly defeated Texas state Senator Arlene Wohlgemuth last election—has colored his attitude toward the administration. In April 2005 a small group of moderate Democrats met with Vice President Richard B. Cheney to discuss whether the White House could collaborate with the minority sometimes, and Edwards took the opportunity to ask him pointedly about two Democratic allies who had recently gone down to defeat.

"Mr. Vice President, Georgia Senator Max Cleland voted for the first two of President Bush's tax cuts, and Republicans ran ads comparing him to Osama Bin Laden," Edwards said. "Congressman Charlie Stenholm worked with the president on his Social Security privatization plan, and Republicans redistricted him out of a seat. Mr. Vice President, where's the incentive for Democrats to work on a bipartisan basis?"

Cheney, Edwards recalled, did not offer much of a response.[34]

This same political tension has affected the entire Texas delegation, which used to have a reputation for fighting together on behalf of the state. DeLay's dogged drive to boost his party's share of Texas House seats has earned him respect among his GOP colleagues, but it has made House Democrats even more hostile.

In the spring of 2003, DeLay hosted a dinner on the second floor of Washington, D.C.'s Union Station for the entire Texas delegation, in which he suggested the two parties work together to draft a new slate of congressional districts. Frost, who at the time was the delegation's longest-serving House member, rose and declared, "We can't work together for the good of the state if you're trying to kill seven of us." DeLay then walked out of the room, saying he had to oversee

33. Edwards interview.
34. Ibid.

late-night speeches on the House floor, which rarely demand senior leaders' supervision.[35]

Redistricting isn't the sole reason districts have become so politically predictable over the past decade: it has amplified underlying demographic trends. Republicans are increasingly choosing to live among Republicans while Democrats are seeking to live alongside Democrats. A recent analysis by the *Austin American-Statesman* found the level of political segregation in American counties rose 47 percent from 1976 to 2000, meaning Americans are now more likely than ever before to live in areas dominated by members of a single party. "Voters on average are less likely today to live in a community that has an even mix of Republican and Democratic voters than at any time since World War II," the paper concluded.[36]

By any measure, House Democrats and Republicans come from different worlds. The average median income in a Southern GOP House district, for example, is $12,000 higher than in a Southern Democratic district.[37] Such disparities, coupled with the fact that voters of color tend to be packed into Democratic districts, create congressional seats that offer a study in contrasts. The twenty-seven most politically lopsided districts in the country—where 2000 presidential candidate Al Gore won at least 77.7 percent of the major-party vote—are Democratic, and in all but two of those districts, minorities make up more than half of the population.[38]

This phenomenon has prompted some Democratic stalwarts like

35. Frost and Edwards interviews.

36. Bill Bishop, "The Schism in U.S. Politics Begins at Home," *Austin American-Statesman*, Apr. 4, 2004.

37. Howard Rosenthal, Spring talk at Princeton University's Woodrow Wilson School of Public Policy on his upcoming book with Columbia University Professor Nolan McCarty and University of Houston Professor Keith T. Poole, "Political Polarization and Income Inequality."

38. Hirsch, "The United States House of Unrepresentatives," 195.

Dingell to mock their GOP counterparts for having a slanted perspective: "These guys only talk to their white supremacist voters."[39] Some Republicans, of course, make equally cutting remarks about the other side. Residential segregation, however, does not fully account for the skewed districts that now make up Congress. Anyone who looks at Pennsylvania's Sixth and Twelfth Districts, whose nicknames "The Dragon" and "The Supine Seahorse" stem from their unusual shapes, can see how political leaders went to extraordinary lengths to craft boundaries favoring one party over another. These oddly designed congressional seats have sapped any unpredictability out of their elections.

Stuart Rothenberg, a political analyst who has been tracking House races for a quarter century, predicts the GOP will hold the House until the end of the decade unless Democrats find some magical silver bullet. "Barring a wave, the House is out of play until the next redistricting," he said. "It's clear that redistricting is the major factor behind the lack of competitiveness."[40]

Moreover, the party leaders appear to have an insatiable appetite for tinkering with state congressional maps long after the Census is done. Federal law requires states to draw new districts every decade to reflect the latest population figures. But members of both parties now see mid-decade redistricting, which used to be practically nonexistent, as a way to exert the utmost political advantage.

Texas and Colorado Republicans proved they could reshape districts in 2003; the Georgia GOP has done the same and now Democrats are spoiling for a fight in states like Illinois, Louisiana, New Mexico, and New York, where they've gained political ground since the start of the decade. (In New York they still need to win the governorship and the state Senate before they can act.)

House Minority Whip Steny Hoyer told reporters in March 2005

39. Dingell interview.

40. Stuart Rothenberg, interview with author, Mar. 10, 2005.

that while he believes redistricting is best done every decade, Democrats would "be foolish to sit on the sidelines and have our heads beaten in and not see what we could do in response. When somebody hits you, you usually put up your arm or you strike back."[41]

Joe Crowley, who has been lobbying members of his delegation to take aim at GOP Representatives Vito Fosella and Sue Kelly, first raised the idea of redoing New York's map just a few days after the 2004 election, in which several Texas Democratic incumbents fell victim to DeLay's redistricting plan. In the light of those results, Crowley reasoned, Democrats in a similarly large state need to exercise their political muscle.

"The other side has dropped a nuclear bomb here," said Crowley, who's counting on his party's likely gubernatorial nominee Elliot Spitzer winning in 2006 along with Democrats retaking control of the state Senate. "There are very few competitive districts in the country to begin with. . . . It forces us to look at other seats out there."[42]

The 2002 and 2003 redistricting efforts have not just boosted the GOP's chances to retain the majority for the rest of the decade, they've fostered extremists on both sides. In a safe district the real election takes place in the dominant party's primary, not in the general election, which means the candidate who caters best to the party base will emerge victorious. This applies to both Democrats and Republicans. James A. Thurber, who directs American University's Center for Congressional and Presidential Studies, quipped that redistricting has skewed House races so much, "If you're from Berkeley you have to declare yourself a Marxist, not a socialist, to get elected."[43]

41. "Hoyer: Dems Should Study Redistricting Opportunities," *CongressDailyAM*, Mar. 2, 2005.

42. Crowley interview.

43. James A. Thurber, interview with author, Jan. 14, 2005.

While centrists in states such as California have pushed for "open primaries" where voters can participate regardless of party affiliation, these efforts have floundered, forcing candidates to adopt more radical positions. As New York University Law School Professor Richard H. Pildes has noted, "Primaries tend to be dominated by the most intensely engaged voters, who typically have more extreme views than median party members. Closed primaries accentuate these effects and are therefore likely to reward candidates more at the extremes of the distribution of office seekers. Open primaries produce candidates closer to the median voter's views, or in more common language, more moderate candidates (and officeholders)."[44]

This polarization stems not only from the kind of voters who participate in a primary, but from the fact that interest groups wield more influence in these contests compared with a general election. In a low-turnout primary—fewer than 10 percent of registered voters usually participate in House primaries—union support is critical to a Democratic candidate, in the same way that support from an anti-abortion or anti-tax group can help a Republican prevail. As a result lawmakers tailor their votes to please these groups, widening the divide between the two parties in Washington.

The most recent round of elections testified to this phenomenon, producing a raft of conservative winners in what had been more marginal Republican seats. A district's shifting political makeup becomes obvious once an incumbent steps down, since that move usually sparks a spirited primary contest in the ruling party. As a result, a district that elected a moderate for years sends a candidate on the right (or in the case of the Democrats, on the left) to Washington as soon as it becomes an open seat.

When Representative Doug Bereuter (R-Neb.)—a critic of the U.S. invasion of Iraq—stepped down, three Republicans vied to take

44. Richard H. Pildes, "The Supreme Court 2003 Term, Foreword: The Constitutionalization of Democratic Politics," *Harvard Law Review* 118, no. 1 (November 2004): 110–111.

his place: state Senate President Curt Bromm, a moderate; former Lincoln City Council member Jeff Fortenberry, an archconservative; and Greg Ruehle, another conservative who had the support of the state's ranching community. Fortenberry managed to mobilize the district's Christian conservatives and home schoolers, winning both the primary and the general election.

Moderate Representative James C. Greenwood's (R-Penn.) retirement in 2004 opened the way for abortion rights opponent Michael G. Fitzpatrick, a local Republican commissioner, to win federal office. Greenwood, who had been one of the House GOP's most prominent abortion rights proponents, warned state Republicans "to take into consideration this is a seat that has never been held by anyone who is not pro-choice," but county Republican leaders picked Fitzpatrick.[45] Greenwood represented a swing district, but Pennsylvania Republicans made sure after the 2000 Census his seat did not become more Democratic. That, coupled with Greenwood's late surprise retirement announcement, ensured Fitzpatrick could go on to win the general contest, despite his conservative views.

Republican Study Committee Executive Director Sheila Cole, whose group represents the conservative wing of the House GOP, saw her organization's ranks swell in the 109th Congress.

"This is a very conservative freshman class," she said.[46]

Some top Democratic and Republican officials have begun to worry that having members from safe seats may undermine their parties' ability to attract broad support because these politicians hear feedback only from one kind of voter. Many lawmakers diligently poll their constituents through town hall meetings and other forums. But they

45. Hal Marcovitz, "Greenwood Blasts Fitzpatrick for Being Pro-Life," *Allentown Morning Call*, July 28, 2004.

46. Sheila Cole, interview with author, Nov. 23, 2005.

often get a single message back from their increasingly homogeneous constituents, who reinforce their preexisting ideological leanings.

Steve Elmendorf, who worked as Richard Gephardt's top aide before serving as one of John Kerry's senior advisers in the 2004 presidential campaign, said House members constantly told him that the Democratic nominee should adopt as liberal positions as possible.

"They don't have as much of a feel for what swing voters think," Elmendorf said. "They think the only way to win a presidential election is to expand the base. That's the only people they talk to, the base."[47]

While House GOP leaders say they felt repeatedly betrayed by Gephardt because he was never able to sway his Caucus into being more cooperative, Elmendorf attributes the Democrats' myopic view of public opinion as hamstringing their leader at times. "At the end of the day the leadership is responsive to the membership," he said. "If they're not getting any pressure from members to compromise, they're not going to do it."

Republicans face the same problem. Ed Gillespie, who headed the Republican National Committee during the 2004 election, has lobbied hard to convince his colleagues that they should make more of an effort to reach out to Latinos and African Americans. Every time he delivers a speech on the subject, GOP senators come up and ask him how they can get involved with the project; their House counterparts tend to walk away.

"House members feel less of a political incentive to do it," Gillespie said. "On the House side there is not as much energy because it's not in their self interest. That is one of the downsides to redistricting, the fact that there are more racially homogeneous districts."[48]

Legislative leaders' insistence on greater unity has only magnified these divisions, turning both camps into regional, rather than national,

47. Elmendorf interview.
48. Ed Gillespie, interview with author, Feb. 17, 2004.

parties. Maverick GOP Senator John McCain (Arizona) said he worries that House GOP leaders are putting Northeastern moderates such as Shays and Representative Rob Simmons (R-Conn.) in a bind.

"There's no doubt discipline is being imposed, it's just a fact of life. The way they operate, the risk is losing people like Chris Shays or Rob Simmons," McCain said. "You can only win so many seats in the South."[49]

Political scientists and good government advocates have fretted for years about House incumbents' reelection advantage. Redistricting has only exacerbated an already disturbing trend. In the 2004 congressional elections, only thirteen seats switched party control, and seven incumbents lost in the general election. In 2002, 82 percent of House members won by a margin of more than 20 percent.[50] As University of Pennsylvania Law School Professor Nathaniel Persily wrote, "current rates of House turnover may equal historic rates of turnover in the Politburo."[51]

Some political pundits have started to wonder if the 2006 congressional elections will represent a break with the past, in which angry voters will be able to oust a bevy of incumbents. This could happen, but even the most optimistic House Democrats acknowledge the current congressional map may impede them from capitalizing on voters' outrage in the fall elections.

With a few exceptions, House members are almost politically unbeatable. This presents an obvious question: how can you expect lawmakers to respond to voters' needs when there's no penalty for ignoring them?

Samuel Issacharoff, a visiting professor at New York University

49. John McCain, interview with author, Jan. 18, 2005.

50. Common Cause press office.

51. Nathaniel Persily, "In Defense of Foxes Guarding Henhouses: The Case for Judicial Acquiescence to Incumbent-Protecting Gerrymandering," *Harvard Law Review* 116, no. 2 (December 2002).

Law School, sees this problem as the worst fallout from the recent redistricting drive.

"Representatives remain faithful to the preferences of the electorate and responsive to shifts in preferences so long as they remain accountable electorally," Issacharoff wrote in a 2002 law review article. "Rather than the selection process being merely a transmission mechanism for expressing the existing preferences of the voters, the power to decide meaningfully among representatives becomes the core of the electorate's democratic rights."[52]

While Issacharoff sees all gerrymanders as stifling voters' ability to influence the political process, he considers bipartisan gerrymanders even more of a threat to democracy. "When there's a partisan gerrymander the voting public, which is being disenfranchised, has a powerful ally, the minority party which got screwed," he said in an interview. "When the parties collude together in the bipartisan gerrymander the voting public has no allies and no chance at a voice."[53]

That's what bothers Blackhawk Country Club resident Shiera Henderson, a Democrat who used to help elect Tauscher but now finds herself in a safely Republican district. Henderson has plenty of animosity toward Pombo, who has used his House Resources Committee chairmanship to seek changes in the Endangered Species Act and other longstanding environmental laws.

"I despise him for what he's doing to the environment," Henderson said. While she was unaware of how state leaders were reconfiguring the district in 2001, she now understands she has little hope of ousting Pombo. "After the fact I realized what they did, and I wasn't happy," she said.[54]

52. Samuel Issacharoff, "Gerrymandering and Political Cartels," *Harvard Law Review* 116, no. 2 (December 2002).

53. Samuel Issacharoff, interview with author, Mar. 4, 2005.

54. Shiera Henderson, interview with author, Jan. 5, 2005.

CHAPTER 6

The Road to Redistricting Reform

As a mapmaker, I can have more of an impact on an election than a campaign, than a candidate. When I, as a mapmaker, have more of an impact on an election than the voters, the system is out of whack.

—GOP consultant David Winston, who drew House districts for the GOP after the 1990 U.S. Census

Those people who sit in Congress should be reflective of the people they represent. It's as simple as that.

—Former New Jersey Governor Richard J. Codey (D)

The current polarization in Washington has left voters disillusioned and many politicians demoralized, prompting some activists to call for change. The question is, what's the best way to do it? Activists and legal scholars have just begun to focus on how to revamp the way states craft congressional districts, raising the first real possibility of change in years.

Lawmakers in twenty-one states, from California to Maryland, have introduced revamping legislation. They are exploring different avenues of change. Schwarzenegger wanted to entrust the job of redistricting to a group of retired judges. Some Florida Democrats are

Epigraphs. David Winston, interview with author, June 9, 2005; Richard J. Codey, interview with author, Apr. 27, 2005.

proposing an independent commission, free of politicians and lobbyists, appointed by Democratic and Republican legislative leaders and the state Supreme Court's chief justice. To gauge these competing proposals, it's worth examining three of the country's most respected redistricting systems, those of Iowa, New Jersey, and Arizona.

Many like to talk about how well Iowa's redistricting process works, in the same way people say Iowans are nice each time the presidential primary season gets under way. In several ways this praise is justified. Since the 1970s, Iowa's system has consistently produced competitive districts that do not disproportionately favor one party or the other. Iowa's approach is straightforward. The nonpartisan Legislative Service Bureau has the job every decade of drawing up both federal and state congressional districts without regard to party registration or to where the incumbents live. They send their plan to the state legislature, which has only the option of voting it up or voting it down without amendment. If the state legislature rejects the plan, the staffers can modify it and send it back. Again, legislators can only accept or refuse it. The bureau can then offer a third plan. This the legislature can amend, but Iowa's representatives have never significantly altered a proposed map. The state Supreme Court only intervenes if the process fails to produce a map, or if a group challenges the final plan in court.

While this process could conceivably lead to gridlock, it rarely does. Iowa lawmakers do not want to appear obstructionist, and they have little incentive to let the courts step in and determine the state's congressional districts. Instead they have traditionally accepted maps like the one the bureau's staff drew after the 2000 Census, which spurred four competitive congressional races.

Iowa's model, however, may not work on a national level. The state has a small number of minorities compared with many other states, so its map makers do not have the same pressures when it comes to meeting Voting Rights Act redistricting requirements. Also, while Iowa has become more politically polarized in recent years, its citizens and lawmakers still retain a sense of pride in their reputation for moderation and fairness. This political culture prevents either party from engaging in brazen attempts to skew the state's redistricting process.

Iowa House members know they can expect a tough race at least once every ten years. In 2000 George W. Bush enjoyed a thirteen-point advantage over Al Gore in Republican Tom Latham's seat. After redistricting the congressman found himself in a district that Bush would have won by just one point.[1] Latham, who had won his old district by 69 percent in 2000, had a tough fight in the next election against Democrat John Norris but held onto his seat with nearly 55 percent of the vote. Iowa Representatives Jim Leach (R) and Leonard Boswell (D) also had tight races in 2002, as did Republican revolutionary Jim Nussle.

New Jersey offers a lesser-known but promising redistricting alternative. The state relies on commissions, equally balanced between the two parties with one tiebreaker appointed by the state Supreme Court, to draw both its state and national legislative districts. Traditionally, the court has appointed a Rutgers or Princeton University political scientist to break the tie. Assuming the tiebreaker is fair and has no hidden partisan allegiance, this system gives both parties an incentive to draw relatively fair maps. During the last round of state redistricting, Princeton University Professor Larry Bartels, who had never even registered to vote, shuttled between Democrats and Republicans for ten days in a conference center on New Jersey's Route 1, trying to strike a deal. Bartels had a simple agenda: "To try to establish a systematic relationship between the amount of support a party received in the state and the [number] of seats that they won."[2]

1. Juliet Eilperin, "Redistricting Rattles In-House Hopes; Some Incumbents Face Unfamiliar Territory; Some Face Off With Each Other," *The Washington Post*, Dec. 31,
2. Bartels interview.

This goal made Republicans nervous, since they controlled the legislature in a Democratic-leaning state. And Democrats were not bashful about lobbying for their cause. Richard J. Codey, who was a state senator at the time but became governor when James McGreevey stepped down in 2004, researched where Bartels went to college and bought him T-shirts and hats from Yale University and the University of California at Berkeley in an effort to curry favor with him. Codey, who occasionally called the professor "Doc," also regularly followed him into the bathroom to chat with Bartels about the two men's children, who are roughly the same age.

"When I saw him in the hallway I never spoke to him about the map, I would talk to him about basketball and the kids," Codey said. "I wanted him to be comfortable with me as a human being."[3]

In the end Bartels approved a map that pleased Democrats, in part because it distributed minority voters more evenly throughout several districts rather than packing them in a few seats, which would have minimized the Democrats' statewide strength. (The Republicans sued to overturn the map under the Voting Rights Act, and lost.) State Republicans were so angry they pushed through initiatives that reduced the Supreme Court's administrative budget, since the court had appointed Bartels, and cut state aid to Princeton by rewriting a state university grant on the basis of how many in-state students they enroll. Bartels noted New Jersey Republicans don't fully grasp how little their retaliatory scheme meant to a rich university like Princeton. "They would have been better off closing the turnpike exit closest to my house," he said.[4]

But the merits of Bartels' focus on partisan fairness became clear after the 2002 election. The Senate, which had been tilted twenty-five to fifteen in the Republicans' favor, ended up evenly split at twenty to twenty. On the House side Democrats, who had been outperforming the Republicans statewide, regained the majority.

3. Codey interview.
4. Bartels interview.

New Jersey's model did not work quite as well when it came to the federal level, where Democratic and Republican incumbents decided they were better off protecting each other than angling for separate maps. Republicans calculated they had already done as well as they could by obtaining six of the state's thirteen House seats, and they wanted to protect junior GOP Representative Michael Ferguson. Democrats, for their part, wanted to make sure Representative Rush Holt retained his Republican-leaning seat based in Princeton. So the two parties essentially outvoted the tiebreaker, Rutgers University political science Professor Alan Rosenthal, and created a map that protected all of New Jersey's incumbents. As Codey observed, "They would meet in Washington, the congressmen, and work it out amongst themselves."[5]

Still, with a few modifications, New Jersey's approach could offer a model that allows political parties to have input into how districts are drawn without letting them dominate the process. With an impartial tiebreaker at the helm of the panel, both parties will devote their energies to drafting maps that reflect the voting preferences of state residents.

Arizona has pioneered yet a third way, after approving a ballot initiative in 2000 aimed at creating fairer and more competitive districts. The state initiative created a five-member citizen commission to draw seats. A state board nominates twenty-five candidates, ten from each party and five that are independent, from which state House and Senate leaders select four appointees. These four men and women then choose the commission's chair from the pool of independent candidates. Steve Lynn, a utilities executive who decided to seek the commission's chairmanship after becoming alienated from both parties, estimated in an interview that he had spent 3,200 hours over the past four years trying to devise a new congressional map for his state.

5. Codey interview.

"I decided I would rather have myself do it than have it done to me," Lynn said. But after spending years in endless meetings and bitter battles over whether the map treated Latinos and American Indians fairly, Lynn has reassessed this philosophy. "In retrospect, maybe I should have had someone else do it."[6]

Arizona gained two seats during the last round of redistricting, which should have made the commission's job easier. But to fulfill what the panel members considered were the requirements under the Voting Rights Act, the commission concentrated the state's Latinos—who tend to vote Democratic—in two congressional districts, which hampered their ability to make the remaining seats competitive. As a result only one seat, the First District, boasts a true contest between the two parties.

"We were all interested in making more competitive seats, but the reality is when you satisfy the Voting Rights Act in a state like Arizona, with a significant minority population, it's very difficult to create competitive districts," Lynn said.[7]

Still, many congressional experts see all three states—Arizona, Iowa, and New Jersey—as possible models when it comes to redistricting. Nine states, for example, are considering legislation that would create an Iowa-like system where political data do not play a role in crafting districts. Creating more seats with competitive general-election contests would give aspiring politicians an incentive to move a little closer to the political center, which in turn could at least foster a more meaningful dialogue on Capitol Hill. That change could reduce the echo-chamber effect that now exists between House members and their like-minded constituents.

"It's not necessary to throw out the baby with the bathwater with redistricting, but simply say we're going to throw out the dirty bath-

6. Steve Lynn, interview with author, Mar. 3, 2005.
7. Ibid.

water, the dirty politicking," said Xavier Becerra, who backs the idea of an independent redistricting commission but wants to keep politicians involved in the process.[8]

The advanced technology election mapmakers employ now has made reform essential.

"We just got too damn good at it," said Tim Storey, a redistricting expert at the nonpartisan National Conference of State Legislatures. Lawmakers, Storey added, "know they're almost bulletproof as incumbents in safe districts. It's totally out of control."[9]

Gingrich, who once touted redistricting as helping foster the GOP's electoral success, now backs any sort of reform plan that involves "citizens who do not have an interest in maximizing leverage."

Under the current system, he reasoned, Democrats "get to rip off the public in the states where they control and protect their incumbents, and we get to rip off the public in the states we control and protect our incumbents, so the public gets ripped off in both circumstances. . . . In the long run, there's a downward spiral of isolation."[10]

Many advocates are calling for a national redistricting system, complete with uniform standards that limit redistricting to once a decade and place a priority on fostering competitiveness, maintaining communities of interest, creating geographically compact districts, and reflecting the state's true political balance. Only two institutions could impose such national standards: the Supreme Court and Congress. Over the past few decades, the Supreme Court has issued rulings in which justices have emphasized the political nature of redistricting, declining to intervene in congressional gerrymanders. It is unclear what kind of map would prompt the Court to step in: a majority of justices indicated in a 2003 ruling that even political gerrymandering

8. Becerra interview.
9. Tim Storey, interview with author, Mar. 3, 2005.
10. Gingrich interview.

can go too far, though they declined to say exactly what constitutes crossing the line.

In a concurring opinion, Justice Anthony Kennedy wrote in that 2003 case, *Vieth v. Jubelirer*, that he would be willing to take a second look at redistricting if he determined it became excessive: "It is not in our tradition to foreclose the judicial process from the attempt to define standards and remedies where it is alleged that a constitutional right is burdened or denied.[11] But he failed to identify any specific judicial remedy to the problem.[12] New York University Law School Professor Richard Pildes argues in a recent law review article that the Court has an obligation to attack "the real incumbent-protection scheme" in our nation's political system, adding, "in the absence of other institutions to check legislative self-entrenchment, courts should use the legitimate constitutional resources available to address this serious risk to the core constitutional value of democratic accountability."[13]

Some incumbents are seeking to revamp the system on their own, though they face formidable opposition. Tennessee Representative John Tanner, a centrist Democrat, introduced legislation in May 2005 that would establish a new national approach to drawing House districts. Under Tanner's bill each state would create an independent redistricting commission of at least five members to draw the state's congressional map just once each decade. The proposal calls for majority and minority state legislative leaders to appoint an even number of commissioners, who would then elect an additional commissioner as chair. Commissioners could not have held elective or

11. *Vieth v. Jubelirer*, 541 U.S. 267 (2004), 1794.

12. Daniel Mach, one of the Jenner & Block attorneys who challenged the Pennsylvania congressional redistricting plan in *Vieth*, said in an interview that the decision left open the possibility that the justices might revisit the issue: "Although no standard has garnered a majority of votes on the Supreme Court, it is clear that, at least in theory, excessive partisan gerrymandering remains subject to judicial scrutiny."

13. Richard H. Pildes, "The Supreme Court 2003 Term, Foreword: The Constitutionalization of Democratic Politics," *Harvard Law Review* 118, no. 1 (2004): 65, 75–76.

appointed office or worked on a campaign for the past four years and would be barred from seeking a House seat in that state for ten years. That would prevent lawmakers from helping craft districts to satisfy their own political ambitions, a strategy that House Republicans such as Thaddeus McCotter (Michigan) and Tom Feeney (Florida) have used to great effect.

In unveiling the bill, Tanner said he wanted to dismantle a process that had "paved the way for partisan extremists unwilling to work cooperatively with others toward the best interest of the country."[14] But the measure is not likely to pass in the near future: four months after Tanner introduced it he had enlisted fifty Democratic co-sponsors but just two Republicans, Phil Gingrey (Georgia) and Zach Wamp.

"I suffer no illusion that this will pass quickly, because you're asking people to give up an enormous amount of power," Tanner said. "I hope this will catch fire from the outside."[15]

Democratic election lawyer Sam Hirsch has drafted a state constitution amendment, loosely modeled on the New Jersey system, which would keep politicians involved in redistricting while ensuring the final map would reflect prevailing political attitudes. Under Hirsch's plan, the tiebreaker on the eleven-member commission would have more votes than all the other members combined, which would block the kind of bipartisan gerrymander that New Jersey congressional incumbents pulled off after the 2000 Census. At the same time it would keep politicians involved in the process, allowing them to provide expertise about campaigning and the electoral nature of individual districts, and would promote plans that emphasize competitiveness and partisan fairness.

Hirsch's proposal appears to be the best way of ensuring that congressional districts reflect the state's partisan balance, as well as

14. John Tanner press release, May 25, 2005.
15. John Tanner, interview with author, Sept. 22, 2005.

the state's racial diversity. "Without clear, tough rules ensuring fairness, commissions will do no better than the politicians have done, and we'll get maps nearly as rotten as the ones we have now," Hirsch said.[16]

Part of the problem in enacting redistricting changes is that the issue does not rank high among voters' priorities. It doesn't even surface among the top six issues Americans want Congress and the president to address, and they dislike initiatives that promote "competitive elections" because they fear these initiatives will translate into even more negative television ads.

"There's not a lot of salience to this issue," said Democratic pollster Celinda Lake, who has conducted surveys on the subject. Voters believe that even if they revamp the redistricting process, "They have the innate feeling politicians will figure out a way around it and undermine the process no matter what."[17]

Tanner has embarked on what he calls "an educational process" to promote his bill, appearing on talk radio shows and discussing it with his constituents in town hall meetings.

"It's sort of like talking about the national debt. Nobody walks around thinking about the national debt. Nobody walks around thinking their district's gerrymandered."[18]

The challenge reformers face was evident on November 8, 2005, when both California's and Ohio's redistricting reform proposals failed by wide margins. California voters rejected Schwarzenegger's plan by a vote of 60 to 40 percent; Ohio's redistricting ballot initiative failed 70 to 30 percent.

The two initiatives fared so badly for two reasons: voters had a hard time deciding if redistricting reform matters; those who did saw it as boosting one party's fortunes over another's. Hirsch analyzed the

16. Juliet Eilperin, "You Can't Have a Great Election without Any Races," *The Washington Post*, Nov. 13, 2005.

17. Celinda Lake, Redistricting Reform Conference, Airlie, Va., June 16, 2005.

18. Tanner interview.

voting returns and found that Californians in counties that favored John Kerry in 2004 opposed the GOP governor's Proposition 77 by a margin of 66 to 34 percent; in Ohio counties that backed George W. Bush opposed the redistricting measure 76 to 24 percent.[19] Former representative David Skaggs, a Colorado Democrat who is championing new redistricting standards at the D.C.-based Council for Excellence in Government, said the results in California and Ohio show that the push for new redistricting methods "has to be clinically non-partisan."[20]

Still, a vocal minority in the House is pushing for more swing districts on the grounds that they force lawmakers to adopt a broader view of the nation's political makeup. Brian Baird, a majority of whose constituents voted for the GOP's presidential, gubernatorial, and senatorial nominees in 2004, has held 250 town hall meetings since winning his seat in 1998.

"It makes your life worse, but it makes you a better person," Baird said. "We are a country of loggers and environmentalists, Christian fundamentalists and liberal agnostics, union activists and anti-union business people. Living in a district where you have to listen to people of diverse perspectives is more indicative of the country as a whole."[21]

And that broad perspective, Tanner argues, gives lawmakers independence from their party leadership once they arrive in Washington.

"I don't give my voting card to Nancy Pelosi, and I don't expect Republicans to give their voting cards to Denny Hastert," he said, as he leant back in a chair just a few yards away from the House floor. "This is not a Democratic or Republican political convention here. This is where the people's business is being done."[22]

19. Eilperin, "You Can't Have a Great Election without Any Races."
20. Ibid.
21. Baird interview.
22. Tanner interview.

CHAPTER 7

How to Restore Civility to the House

When we get done we're not going back to the fair way of doing things. Democrats will say [to Republicans] you did it, now you bastards enjoy it.

—John D. Dingell (D-Mich.), on how some Democrats would like to rule the House if they regained the majority

Billy Tauzin didn't realize how much party relations had deteriorated until he was convalescing from intestinal cancer in 2004 at his ranch in Batesville, Texas, watching C-SPAN.

"It was so sad to watch it," he said, recalling how he stared at his colleagues as they tore each other apart on the House floor.[1]

Lying in his bed, Tauzin wrote pages on pages of notes in heavy black ink on how to improve relations between the Democrats and Republicans, the two camps that had fostered his political ascent. Some of the ideas were a bit far-fetched—civility classes for lawmakers, a public "Hall of Shame" aimed at embarrassing troublesome

Epigraph. Dingell interview.

1. Tauzin interview.

members—but others less so. Tauzin called for Republicans to enforce the rule that prohibits members from questioning one another's motives on the House floor, one that politicians flout constantly. He suggested that leaders make time for lawmakers to engage in impromptu floor debates, so they can participate in a genuine discussion rather than the scripted exchanges that stem from staff-written speeches. Members need to spend more time socializing with each other, he wrote, so they can discover redeeming qualities in their partisan opponents.

Tauzin keeps his observations in a manila envelope in his PhRMA offices in Washington, where he shared them with me one summer afternoon in 2005. No one from the House leadership has ever perused them.

Party leaders, he said, have spent years telling the rank and file "there was evil on the other side."[2] Only a major overhaul, Tauzin reasoned, could restore a sense of comity to the broken institution he watched with distaste from his sickbed.

Many current and former lawmakers have ideas on how to make, in the words of Gingrich, "a more humane House." Open up the rules process, for example, so dissenters in both the minority and the majority can amend legislation. Allow time for floor debate so members have a chance to exchange ideas, and perhaps sway each other on occasion. Force members to stay in town more often—Brian Baird thinks the House should be in session five days a week for three weeks in a row, with one week off—so members can get to know each other and have more flexibility to meet with constituents back home as well as in D.C.

By making Democrats and Republicans spend more time together, lawmakers might establish the sort of rapport that often

2. Ibid.

underpins substantive policy accords. For a period after the September 11 attacks, Bush brought in the top Republican and Democratic House and Senate leaders for a weekly meeting, and those sessions helped smooth the passage of several key bills. The president abandoned the practice in 2002, however, and Hastert and Pelosi now meet only a handful of times each year. Most of the time when Pelosi wants to communicate with the Speaker, she drafts a letter and releases it to the press.

"We've got to increase communication on the leadership level, so we can learn how to disagree without being disagreeable," said Representative Ron Kind (D-Wis.).[3]

Democrats have a favorite proposal for change: put their party back in charge. But that won't serve as a panacea for the House's current ills. Richard Gephardt would like to believe his party would behave differently from Republicans—and their Democratic predecessors—if they won back the House, but he can't be sure. "It's an open question," he said. "I would hope we would not do what Republicans did."[4]

A few bipartisan coalitions have begun pushing for reform, but these efforts have yet to bear fruit. Like Tauzin, the founders of the Center Aisle Caucus have suggested that lawmakers from opposing sides participate in informal policy briefings and after-hours talks to spur a sincere exchange of ideas. "This is not holding hands singing Kumbaya," said Center Aisle Caucus Co-chair Steve Israel. "We don't have time to debate."[5]

Republicans have initiated their own effort to foster civility; Rules Committee Chairman David Drier has asked Representative Shelley Moore Capito (R-W.Va.) to establish a task force on the subject. But even Capito, a popular Republican who displays a bit of a rebellious streak at times, couldn't resist mocking her leadership-appointed role

3. Ron Kind, interview with author, July 7, 2005.
4. Gephardt interview.
5. Israel interview.

during a 2005 commencement speech at Hampden-Sydney, an all-male liberal arts college in Virginia. "Hampden-Sydney has forged you into good citizens," Capito told the students. "In Congress, I have been appointed to head a task force on civility. As a measure of my success and of how Congress has been going lately, I can tell you to date I am still this task force's only member. Our Congress could use a good dose of Hampden-Sydney civility."[6]

Dreier said in an interview two months after Capito's speech that he had "no excuse" for not assembling the task force quicker: "I've been buried in a lot of things. It's still something I want to do."[7]

But as of October 2005, Dreier had yet to move on the task force. "She's still its only member, and she's still using that same joke," said Capito spokesman R. C. Hammond.[8]

The past two decades of political polarization—starting with Indiana's Bloody Eighth and Robert Bork's failed Supreme Court nomination, running through the Republican Revolution, President Clinton's impeachment, and Tom DeLay's current ethics fight—throw into question whether House Republicans and Democrats can collaborate for a sustained period of time. Perhaps the period when they worked together was an aberration, since many Republicans were convinced they would remain permanently in the minority. The parties were more ideologically diverse, so it made more sense for members to work across the aisle. And Democrats enjoyed a wide enough margin of control that they could afford to allow for some defections among their ranks. Current Republican leaders, by contrast, still live in fear of losing control despite their obvious electoral advantage. Bill Thomas described the situation of House Republicans today as like

6. Shelley Moore Capito, commencement address, Hampden-Sydney College, May 8, 2005.

7. Dreier interview.

8. R. C. Hammond, interview with author, Oct. 13, 2005.

being "in the military, where we all have to stick together or we'll be killed."[9]

Or perhaps it's simply that Republicans used confrontational tactics so effectively to win power in 1994, they've convinced both themselves and their opponents to adopt that strategy indefinitely. House members on both sides are obsessed with electoral success, because they know how much better it is to serve in the majority. As a result it's hard to convince them to shift course once they've identified a winning strategy. Princeton University Professor Howard Rosenthal likes to joke that he and his co-author, University of Houston Professor Keith Poole, asked in their 1984 political polarization article "when it would end, and it still hasn't ended."[10]

But victory at all costs makes it nearly impossible to forge a legislative consensus. "When you have a polarized political environment you're having a discourse of contradiction," David Winston said. "Contradiction does not get to resolution."[11] Instead lawmakers are talking past each other, leaving little room for a substantive policy discussion.

At times party leaders appear convinced that they're more conciliatory than they really are. Tom DeLay said during a June 2005 press conference that the fact that a few dozen Democrats had joined with his party on key votes meant GOP leaders had attracted "strong bipartisan support for what we've done,"[12] though the legislative record suggests otherwise. According to a *Washington Post* analysis of close votes over the past decade, the instances where fifty Democrats joined at least two hundred Republicans occurred rarely, from 8 to 10 percent of the time.[13]

9. Thomas interview.
10. Howard Rosenthal, interview with author, Mar. 9, 2005.
11. Winston interview.
12. Tom DeLay weekly press conference, June 28, 2005.
13. Derek Willis, *The Washington Post* research database editor. Analysis of votes decided by less than fifty votes.

Chipping away at the power of incumbency and of extreme partisans—by shifting the way districts are drawn—will not produce instant results. The parties have drifted apart, and their members are still nursing the wounds of a two-decade-long political battle. It will take years to rebuild relationships on Capitol Hill. But many representatives, particularly those focused on legislative substance, are seeking a rapprochement.

Thomas, who used to hail from a more competitive district and immerses himself deeply in policy matters, said he wishes he had more of a chance to incorporate Democratic amendments into his committee's bills. Baird, who likes to point to the signed legislation on his office walls, said he occasionally recoils when he watches his colleagues rush into the House chamber for a vote and immediately seek out the Democratic aide who is making a thumbs-up or thumbs-down sign on the bill at hand: "On some issues you can't just come down and say, 'How is someone telling me to vote?'"[14]

Representative David Price (D-N.C.), who taught political science and public policy for years at Duke University, said he and other Democrats are not simply complaining about their own plight when they criticize the way Republicans run the House. "It does go beyond merely a personal grievance and speaks to the institution's strength and capacity," Price said. "It's a general weakening of the institution's ability to take on hard issues, which is an essential component of the institution's strength."[15]

To underscore this point, Price likes to conduct a thought experiment with audiences back home. He harkens back to the 1990 budget accord between congressional Democrats and President Bush's father, an accord that House conservatives blasted but which ultimately reduced the federal deficit by $500 billion. "That was probably one of the most important things we did in terms of the entire

14. Baird interview.
15. David Price, interview with author, Feb. 10, 2005.

decade," Price said. "Can you begin to imagine that taking place in Congress today? The capacity just doesn't exist."[16]

Congress is not at a standstill: in the past few years alone, it has authorized and funded a war overseas, approved multiple tax cuts, and added a major new benefit to Medicare. But all of these measures required divisive votes, and lawmakers have yet to reach a consensus on pressing issues, such as how to sustain the nation's Social Security system and rein in a ballooning deficit.

Even national disasters no longer unite lawmakers. After Hurricane Katrina hit the Gulf Coast, the two parties bickered not only over how the federal government handled the catastrophe but over how to assess the emergency response. Democrats called for an independent inquiry modeled on the commission that examined the September 11, 2001, terrorist attacks on the United States; Republicans instead established a joint House-Senate committee, controlled by the GOP, to investigate the matter. Republican National Committee Chairman Ken Mehlman chided Nancy Pelosi and Senate Minority Leader Harry Reid (D-Nev.) for questioning the federal government's handling of the disaster: "While countless Americans are pulling together to lend a helping hand, Nancy Pelosi and Harry Reid are pointing fingers in a shameless attempt to pull us apart."[17]

While the task of reviving representative democracy in the House may seem daunting, every American has an interest in seeing it succeed. Bipartisanship has its disadvantages—recent multibillion-dollar giveaways in the energy and highway bills to powerful interests exemplify the pitfalls of cross-party collaboration—but both parties could benefit from working together on fairer terms. Demoralized Democrats as well as many voters are eager to have more of a voice in

16. Ibid.

17. Jonathan Weisman and Amy Goldstein, "Bush Requests $51.8 Billion More for Relief," *The Washington Post*, Sept. 8, 2005.

federal policymaking. Israel admitted in an interview that at times the sniping "makes you wonder, what am I doing here?"[18]

The GOP majority also has a stake in the process, since a deep chasm between Republican leaders and the public could imperil the party's long-term electoral future. Approval ratings for Congress have dipped recently to their lowest levels since the GOP took control, a bad omen for any ruling party. A *Washington Post-ABC News* tracking poll on August 28, 2005, reported that when voters were asked what they thought of Congress, 37 percent approved and 59 percent disapproved. By comparison, that same poll showed on April 22, 2001, that 58 percent of voters approved and 33 percent disapproved of Congress.[19]

And a *USA Today*/CNN/Gallup poll in October 2005 showed that when respondents listed the factors that will most influence their vote in the 2006 congressional elections, government corruption ranked as high up in Americans' minds as terrorism, with a 45 percent response rate. Corruption surpassed the war in Iraq and the economy as a key issue for voters.[20]

Democrats are trying to take advantage of this phenomenon, portraying Republicans as just as unethical and deaf to voters' needs as the congressional leaders who ruled the House in the 1980s and early 1990s. The day a Texas grand jury indicted Tom DeLay for the first time, Pelosi said, "The criminal indictment of Majority Leader Tom DeLay is the latest example that Republicans in Congress are plagued by a culture of corruption at the expense of the American people."[21] Gingrich could have written the script himself, along with the "Road

18. Israel interview.

19. *The Washington Post-ABC News* tracking poll, Aug. 28, 2005, and Apr. 22, 2001. The current poll numbers for Congress are not quite as low as they were just before Democrats lost control of the chamber. At that point, on Oct. 31, 1994, respondents gave Congress a rating of 21 percent approval, and 72 percent disapproval.

20. *USA Today*/CNN/Gallup poll, Oct. 25, 2005.

21. Smith, "DeLay Indicted in Campaign Finance Probe."

to Reform" banners Democrats now display at their Capitol Hill press conferences.

After all, Republicans managed to mobilize voters across the country, unseat a sitting Speaker, and wrest control of a branch of government from an entrenched majority by convincing Americans that Democrats were out of touch with ordinary citizens. Bill Paxon still fondly recalls the time when in 1998 he showed up for a town hall meeting at eight o'clock in the morning at a Denny's restaurant in Amherst, New York, only to encounter one of his constituents quoting a speech that Newt Gingrich had delivered earlier that morning. At first he thought it "was sort of strange" that his constituent had been up at two in the morning watching Gingrich's speech on C-SPAN, until he saw "four other people in the audience were shaking their heads. They had heard the same speech. . . . People in my hometown can follow in real time what's happening in Congress."[22]

Paxon is right. Regular Americans are more aware now than ever about what happens in Washington, D.C. But if their votes don't influence who makes it there to determine policy, then what use is this newfound knowledge?

Mickey Edwards has devised a simple political test for his former colleagues: "The single most important defining quality of a representative, or mediated, democracy, is that the people, through their representatives, indirectly but powerfully, determine the laws they live under, the wars they fight, and the very shape of the society they live in."[23] It is a test the House is failing.

Unfortunately, the men and women who are best equipped to make the House more open and accountable—the top leaders from both parties—appear the least inclined to do it. As a sign of how reluctant they are to engage in this debate, the House's top five leaders—Hastert, Pelosi, DeLay, Hoyer, and Blunt—were the only

22. Paxon interview.

23. Edwards, "Checks and Balances, Perspectives on American Democracy."

elected officials I approached who declined to be interviewed for this book.

"There is no institutional support for restoring comity and respect and order," Tauzin said. "It's going to take some cataclysmic voter reaction."[24]

Gephardt offered a similar assessment. "The only way to get back to a more collaborative atmosphere is for the people to demand it. The voters will ultimately judge if they're getting what they want, or what they need."[25]

For all its flaws, the House of Representatives is an institution that deserves saving. Even on its worst days, serving as a member there is an exceptional post, full of possibility. These men and women make decisions on a daily basis that can have a huge effect on individuals' lives, whether they receive Social Security checks, what kind of health care they may get in times of need, or how well the United States can cope with a future terrorist attack or natural disaster.

Americans had high expectations of their lawmakers when they first formed Congress in the late 1700s. Thomas Rice, a Massachusetts physician and state senator, wrote his congressman George Thatcher on May 2, 1789, that he "shall take the Liberty to suggest to you my ardent wish for the prosperity of my country which under Providence depends in a great measure on the present Congress. Great things are expected from them, and from the known Abilities and integrity of the Gentlemen who compose that honorable body. 'tis expected those great things will be done in the wisest and best manner."[26] But these lawmakers also realized Congress would never be better than the people who served there. On May 12, 1789, New

24. Tauzin interview.

25. Gephardt interview.

26. Charlene Bangs Bickford and Kenneth R. Bowling, eds., *Documentary History of the First Federal Congress of the United States of America, 4 March 1789–3 March 1791* (Baltimore: Johns Hopkins University Press, 1992), 429.

Hampshire senator Paine Wingate wrote congressional minister Jeremy Belknap: "Dear Sir I fear that your expectation, and that of the public in general, will be raised *too high*, respecting the new government. You will remember that Congress is but a collective body of men, men of like passions, subject to local prejudices & those bypasses which in some measure are inseparable from human nature. I say this not to lessen their true merit, for I esteem them in general as very worthy characters; but not without considerable imperfections."[27] In the end, voters must ask their imperfect representatives to improve an extraordinary but flawed political system.

When asked if he would ever consider quitting the House to pursue a different career, Barney Frank repeated the joke the late comedian Henny Youngman told when asked the question, "How's your wife?"

"Compared to what?" came Frank's response. "What position in society would give me more opportunity to influence the things I care about?"[28]

27. Ibid., 535.
28. Frank interview.

Elkanah Tisdale's original "The Gerrymander," as it appeared in the *Boston Gazette*, March 26, 1812

AFTERWORD

> This is the people's Congress. And most of the people don't care which party controls it; what they want is a government that is limited, honest, accountable, and responsive to their needs. The moment a majority forgets this lesson, it begins writing itself a ticket to minority status.
>
> —House Minority Leader John Boehner (R-Ohio), on the Opening Day of the 110th Congress

Shortly before midnight on November 7, 2006 Nancy Pelosi took to the podium at the Capitol Hyatt to address the hundreds of ebullient Democrats. After a dozen years in the wilderness Democrats had finally won back control of Congress and they were both literally and figuratively drunk at the prospect of their newfound power, clinking beer bottles and chanting, "Nancy! Nancy!" and "Speaker! Speaker!" at the 66-year old woman standing before them

Pelosi beamed, and told the crowd she and her colleagues were prepared to chart a new way of governing in Washington.

"The American people voted for a new direction to restore civility and bipartisanship in Washington D.C. And Democrats promise to

Epigraph. John Boehner, Opening Day floor speech, Jan. 7, 2007.

work together in a bipartisan way for all Americans," she said. "We are prepared to govern. And we will do so working together with the administration and the Republicans in Congress in partnership, not in partisanship."[1]

Pelosi's gracious tone posed a stark contrast from the message she had delivered to Democrats while they were in the minority: for months she had warned them they would pay a price for cooperating with the other party. But she and her top lieutenants said they were serious about treating the minority with greater respect than the GOP had given them.

Just minutes before Pelosi delivered her election-night victory speech, Representative John D. Dingell (D-Mich.) said in an interview, "She will run the House the way it should be, with fairness, civility and courtesy."[2] Five weeks later Representative Charlie Rangel (D-N.Y.) told the *Washington Post*, "One of my biggest jobs is to convince Democrats that it's not in our best interests to get even if we want to get something done. I'm convinced the Republican losses wasn't because of this country's love of Democrats. It was the frustration with the war, with Katrina, with corruption. Now, we have a two-year window."[3]

The Democrats followed though on Pelosi's promise during their first two days back in power. As part of their opening business on January 4, 2007 Democrats adopted tighter ethics rules in the House, banning gifts and meals from lobbyists and severely restricting privately funded travel for lawmakers and their aides. The next day they guaranteed the minority several key rights, including control of at least one-third of committee budgets and adequate time to review any bill or committee report headed to the floor for a vote.

1. Nancy Pelosi's election-night victory speech, Nov. 7, 2006.

2. John D. Dingell, interview with author, Nov. 7, 2006.

3. Wil Haygood, "Ways and Means: After 35 Years in the House, Charlie Rangel Has the Power. But There Are Still Taxing Times Ahead for the Man From Harlem," *Washington Post*, Dec. 14, 2006.

The move was not only the right thing to do, it was smart politics. As much as anything else, the 2006 mid-term elections reminded lawmakers that the battle for national political dominance in the United States remains a fight for the center. Republicans had forgotten that, along with their vows to reform Congress and be more accountable to the public than their Democratic predecessors. The scandals that engulfed GOP lawmakers in the final weeks before the election—including former Representative Mark Foley's (R-Fla.) inappropriate overtures to underage male pages and the FBI probe of former Representative Curt Weldon's (R-Penn.) push for government contracts that may have aided his daughter's business—highlighted how much the GOP had drifted from its reformist roots. As House Minority Leader John Boehner (R-Ohio) noted during his speech before handing over the gavel to Pelosi with a kiss and a hug, "If there is one lesson that stands out from our party's time in the majority, it is this: a congressional majority is simply a means to an end. The value of a majority lies not in the chance to wield great power, but in the chance to use limited power to do great things."[4]

Now Democrats have a second chance at governing, with a 233–202 margin of control in the House. Their 30-seat pickup this past election reflected a deep wave of voter resentment, both over the war in Iraq and over GOP leaders' style of running the House. In many cases Democrats managed to overcome gerrymandering to unseat entrenched GOP incumbents such as House Resources Committee Chairman Richard M. Pombo (Calif.), who told me in June 2006 that he was confident he would retain his seat because his party enjoyed a 7-point advantage there. This same tide swept away Republican lawmakers in skewed districts in Indiana, Pennsylvania, and New York, leaving 22 GOP incumbents out of a job.

After all, all the sophisticated map making and get-out-the-vote efforts cannot succeed if voters cannot stand the men and women

4. Boehner, Opening Day floor speech.

who benefit from such manipulation. Pennsylvania Republicans had gone to extraordinary lengths to their House members during the last round of redistricting yet four of them—Michael Fitzpatrick, Melissa Hart, Don Sherwood, and Curt Weldon—lost their seats in 2006. On the Senate side, one GOP strategist confessed on Election Day that his party's sophisticated computer programs could only do so much to help embattled incumbent Montana Senator Conrad Burns. "The good news is we're turning out GOP voters," he said. "The bad news is we're pretty sure 20 percent of them hate Burns."[5] Burns lost the race.

Now that Democrats have emerged victorious Pelosi and her colleagues would be wise to look at the 2006 National Election Pool exit poll conducted by Edison/Mitofsky, in which 47 percent of respondents identified themselves as moderate, 32 percent as conservative and 20 percent as liberal. As former House Majority Leader Richard K. Armey (R-Tex.) predicted shortly before the election, the biggest challenge the new Democrats may face is how to handle the demands of left-leaning interest groups that have been shut out of policy making for a dozen years.[6] And when House Democratic leaders decided to push through their opening-day agenda without allowing Republicans a chance to offer substitutes on the House floor, they demonstrated that they had not quite broken with a past which prized legislative victories above consensus.[7]

While many political pundits highlighted a handful of moderate Democrats who managed to unseat GOP incumbents, such as Indiana sheriff Brad Elsworth and former Redskins football player Heath Shuler, the fact is there may be fewer centrists in the 110th Congress than the 109th Congress. Liberals defeated House Republicans in states ranging from New Hampshire to Kentucky, and the defeat of

5. GOP operative who asked not to be identified, interview with author, Nov. 7, 2006.

6. Richard K. Armey, interview with the author, Nov. 1 2006.

7. Lindsay Layton and Juliet Eilperin, "xx," *Washington Post*, Jan. 2, 2007.

eight of the House's most centrist Republicans in 2006 means there are fewer moderates in the GOP now than in any time during the past century.[8]

And while Democrats were able to capitalize on a wave of voter anger to topple several entrenched incumbents, some of them recognize that under normal circumstances they would not have managed to overcome the advantage many of these lawmakers had locked in through redistricting. A handful of centrists are still hoping to banish gerrymandering from the political process: in December 2006 California Governor Arnold Schwarzenegger (R) offered a new redistricting reform plan that, unlike his previous proposal, called for a bipartisan citizens' commission that would not be biased in favor of his own party.

Representative John Tanner (D-Tenn.) is still trying to push his proposal on Capitol Hill as well. "The current redistricting process amounts to a power grab by those in power and bypasses the voters," he said. "The result is ideologically extreme representation that ignores the political center and an unwillingness to work with others to find realistic solutions to the country's problems."[9]

It may be that Washington power brokers have finally tired of the polarization and high-handed tactics that have dominated Capitol Hill for more than a decade. In a speech at Indiana University Purdue University Indianapolis a month after the 2006 election, New Democratic Network president Simon Rosenberg suggested the election's outcome ended a quarter century of conservative ascendancy pioneered by Ronald Reagan. Instead, he said, it marked the beginning of "an era of new politics," in which the two parties could fight on a

8. Zachary A. Goldfarb, "Democratic Wave in Congress Further Erodes Moderation in GOP," *Washington Post*, Dec. 7, 2006. According to the scale developed by University of California, San Diego political science professor Keith T. Poole and New York University politics professor Howard Rosenthal, 30 years ago nearly half of all Republicans were moderate, compared to 3 percent in the 110th Congress.

9. Email from John Tanner, Dec. 20, 2006.

level playing field to win the loyalty of an increasingly diverse American electorate.[10] The key to winning in this new era involves ditching scorched-earth tactics and rigged congressional maps in favor of innovative policy proposals and high-tech voter outreach. All it will take is a few bold politicians who understand building an enduring majority in the twenty-first century means breaking the corrosive cycle that has dominated national politics in the twilight of the twentieth.

10. Simon Rosenberg, "Enlarging the Tent in 2006 and 2008," The Seventh Bulen Symposium on American Politics, Indiana University Purdue University Indianapolis, Dec. 18, 2006.

APPENDIX A

Key Congressional Players

House Member	*Dates of Service*	*Leadership Post or Committee Chairmanship*
Richard K. Armey (R-Tex.)	Jan. 3, 1985–Jan. 3, 2003	Former Majority Leader
Brian Baird (D-Wash.)	Jan. 6, 1999–Present	
James Barcia (D-Mich.)	Jan. 3, 1993–Jan. 3, 2003	
Joe Barton (R-Tex.)	Jan. 3, 1985–Present	Energy and Commerce Committee Chairman
Charlie Bass (R-N.H.)	Jan. 4, 1995–Present	
Melissa Bean (D-Ill.)	Jan. 4, 2005–Present	
Xavier Becerra (D-Calif.)	Jan. 5, 1993–Present	
Doug Bereuter (R-Neb.)	Jan. 3, 1979–Aug. 31, 2004	
Howard Berman (D-Calif.)	Jan. 3, 1983–Present	
Thomas Bliley (R-Va.)	Jan. 3, 1981–Jan. 3, 2001	Former Energy and Commerce Committee Chairman
Roy Blunt (R-Mo.)	Jan. 6, 1997–Present	Acting Majority Leader
Sherwood Boehlert (R-N.Y.)	Jan. 3, 1983–Present	Science Committee Chairman
John Boehner (R-Ohio)	Jan. 3, 1991–Present	Education and Workforce Committee Chairman
David Bonior (D-Mich.)	Jan. 3, 1977–Jan. 3, 2003	Former Minority Whip
Leonard Boswell (D-Iowa)	Jan. 6, 1997–Present	
Barbara Boxer (D-Calif.)	Jan. 3, 1983–Jan. 3, 1993	
Allen Boyd (D-Fla.)	Jan. 6, 1997–Present	
Sherrod Brown (D-Ohio)	Jan. 5, 1993–Present	
Sam Brownback (R.-Kans.)	Jan. 4, 1995–Nov. 7, 1996	
Eric Cantor (R-Va.)	Jan. 3, 2001–Present	Acting Majority Whip
Shelley Moore Capito (R-W.Va.)	Jan. 3, 2001–Present	
Lois Capps (D-Calif.)	Mar. 10, 1998–Present	
Dennis Cardoza (D-Calif.)	Jan. 7, 2003–Present	

House Member	*Dates of Service*	*Leadership Post or Committee Chairmanship*
Jon Christensen (R-Neb.)	Jan. 4, 1995–Jan. 3, 1999	
Tom Coburn (R-Okla.)	Jan. 4, 1995–Jan. 3, 2001	
Gary Condit (D-Calif.)	Sept. 12, 1989–Jan. 3, 2003	
Jim Costa (D-Calif.)	Jan. 4, 2005–Present	
Philip Crane (R-Ill.)	Nov. 25, 1969–Jan. 3, 2005	
Joseph Crowley (D-N.Y.)	Jan. 6, 1999–Present	
Thomas M. Davis III (R-Va.)	Jan. 4, 1995–Present	Former National Republican Congressional Committee Chairman
Tom DeLay (R-Tex.)	Jan. 3, 1985–Present	Former Majority Leader
Lincoln Diaz–Balart (R-Fla.)	Jan. 5, 1993–Present	
John D. Dingell (D-Mich.)	Dec. 13, 1955–Present	Energy and Commerce Committee, ranking member
Cal Dooley (D-Calif.)	Jan. 3, 1991–Jan. 3, 2005	
David Dreier (R-Calif.)	Jan. 5, 1981–Present	Rules Committee Chairman
Chet Edwards (D-Tex.)	Jan. 3, 1991–Present	
Mickey Edwards (R-Okla.)	Jan. 3, 1977–Jan. 3, 1993	Former GOP Policy Committee Chairman
Anna G. Eshoo (D-Calif.)	Jan. 5, 1993–Present	
Tom Feeney (R-Fla.)	Jan. 7, 2003–Present	
Michael Ferguson (R-N.J.)	Jan. 3, 2001–Present	
Bob Filner (D-Calif.)	Jan. 5, 1993–Present	
Michael G. Fitzpatrick (R-Penn.)	Jan. 4, 2005–Present	
Jeff Flake (R-Ariz.)	Jan. 3, 2001–Present	
Mark Foley (R-Fla.)	Jan. 4, 1995–Present	
Tom Foley (D-Wash.)	Jan. 3, 1965–Jan. 3, 1995	Former Speaker
Barney Frank (D-Mass.)	Jan. 5, 1981–Present	
Trent Franks (R-Ariz.)	Jan. 7, 2003–Present	
Martin Frost (D-Tex.)	Jan. 3, 1979–Jan. 3, 2005	Former Democratic Campaign Committee Chairman
Elton Gallegly (R-Calif.)	Jan. 6, 1987–Present	
Richard A. Gephardt (D-Mo.)	Jan. 3, 1977–Jan. 3, 2005	Former Minority Leader
Phil Gingrey (R-Ga.)	Jan. 7, 2003–Present	
Newt Gingrich (R-Ga.)	Jan. 3, 1979–Jan. 3, 1999	Former Speaker
Henry Gonzalez (D-Tex.)	Nov. 4, 1969–Jan. 3, 1999	Former Banking, Finance and Urban Affairs Committee Chairman
Porter Goss (R-Fla.)	Jan. 3, 1989–Sept. 23, 2004	Former Permanent Select Committee on Intelligence Chairman
Willis Gradison (R-Ohio)	Jan. 3, 1975–Jan. 31, 1993	
James C. Greenwood (R-Penn.)	Jan. 3, 1993–Jan. 3, 2005	
Steve Gunderson (R-Wis.)	Jan. 3, 1981–Jan. 3, 1997	

House Member	*Dates of Service*	*Leadership Post or Committee Chairmanship*
Gil Gutknecht (R-Minn.)	Jan. 4, 1995–Present	
Ralph Hall (R-Tex.)	Jan. 5, 1981–Present	
J. Dennis Hastert (R-Ill.)	Jan. 6, 1987–Present	Speaker
Richard "Doc" Hastings (R-Fla.)	Jan. 4, 1995–Present	
Joel Hefley (R-Colo.)	Jan. 6, 1987–Present	Former Committee on Standards of Official Conduct Chairman
Rush Holt (D-N.J.)	Jan. 6, 1999–Present	
Steve Horn (R-Calif.)	Jan. 3, 1993–Jan. 3, 2003	
Steny Hoyer (D-Md.)	May 19, 1981–Present	Minority Whip
Henry J. Hyde (R-Ill.)	Jan. 14, 1975–Present	International Relations Committee Chairman
Steve Israel (D-N.Y.)	Jan. 3, 2001–Present	
Nancy Johnson (R-Conn.)	Jan.3, 1983–Present	Former Committee on Standards of Official Conduct Chairman
Sam Johnson (R-Tex.)	May 18, 1991–Present	
Timothy V. Johnson (R-Ind.)	Jan. 3, 2001–Present	
Walter B. Jones (R-N.C.)	Jan. 4, 1995–Present	
Patrick Kennedy (D-R.I.)	Jan. 4, 1995–Present	Former Democratic Congressional Campaign Committee Chairman
Ron Kind (D-Wis.)	Jan. 6, 1997–Present	
Peter King (R-N.Y.)	Jan. 5, 1993–Present	
Ray LaHood (R-Ill.)	Jan. 4, 1995–Present	
Tom Latham (R-Iowa)	Jan. 4, 1995–Present	
James Leach (R-Iowa)	Jan. 4, 1977–Present	Former Banking and Financial Services Committee Chairman
John LeBoutillier (R-N.Y.)	Jan. 3, 1981–Jan. 3, 1983	
John Lesinski Jr. (R-Mich.)	Jan. 3, 1951–Jan. 3, 1965	
Jerry Lewis (R-Calif.)	Jan. 15, 1979–Present	Appropriations Committee Chairman
John Lewis (D-Ga.)	Jan. 6, 1987–Present	
John Linder (R-Ga.)	Jan. 5, 1993–Present	
Robert Livingston (R-La.)	Aug. 27, 1977–Feb. 28, 1999	Former Speaker-designate
Connie Mack (R-Fla.)	Jan. 3, 1983–Jan. 3, 1989	Former GOP Conference Chairman
James Madison (R-Va.)	Mar. 4, 1789–Mar. 3, 1797	
Frank McCloskey (D-Ind.)	Jan. 3, 1983–Jan. 3, 1995	Because Frank McCloskey's seat was contested, he served from Jan. 3, 1983, to Jan. 3, 1985, and then was reseated on May 1, 1985.
Thaddeus McCotter (R-Mich.)	Jan. 7, 2003–Present	

House Member	*Dates of Service*	*Leadership Post or Committee Chairmanship*
Jim McCrery (R-La.)	April 16, 1988–Present	
Scott McInnis (R-Colo.)	Jan. 3, 1993–Jan. 3, 2005	
Gregory Meeks (D-N.Y.)	Feb. 3, 1998–Present	
Robert H. Michel (R-Ill.)	Jan. 3, 1957–Jan. 3, 1995	Former Minority Leader
Candice Miller (R-Mich.)	Jan. 7, 2003–Present	
George Miller (D-Calif.)	Jan. 14, 1975–Present	Education and Workforce Committee, ranking member
Norm Mineta (D-Calif.)	Jan. 3, 1975–Oct. 10, 1995	Former Public Works and Transportation Committee Chairman
G. V. "Sonny" Montgomery (D-Miss.)	Jan. 3, 1967–Jan. 3, 1997	
Carlos Moorhead (R-Calif.)	Jan. 3, 1973–Jan. 3, 1997	
James P. Moran (D-Va.)	Jan. 3, 1991–Present	
John P. "Jack" Murtha (D-Penn.)	Feb. 5, 1974–Present	
Sue Myrick (R-S.C.)	Jan. 4, 1995–Present	
Jerrold Nadler (D-N.Y.)	Nov. 3, 1992–Present	
William Natcher (D-Ky.)	Aug. 1, 1953–Mar. 29, 1994	Former Appropriations Committee Chairman
Anne Northup (R-Ky.)	Jan. 6, 1997–Present	
Jim Nussle (R-Iowa)	Jan. 3, 1991–Present	Budget Committee Chairman
David Obey (D-Wis.)	April 1, 1969–Present	Appropriations Committee, ranking member
Thomas P. "Tip" O'Neill (D-Mass.)	Jan. 3, 1953–Jan. 3, 1987	Former Speaker
C. L. "Butch" Otter (R-Idaho)	Jan. 3, 2001–Present	
Bill Paxon (R-N.Y.)	Jan. 3, 1989–Jan. 3, 1999	Former National Republican Congressional Committee Chairman
Nancy Pelosi (D-Calif.)	June 2, 1987–Present	Minority Leader
Collin Peterson (D-Minn.)	Jan. 3, 1991–Present	Agriculture Committee, ranking member
Charles "Chip" Pickering (R-Miss.)	Jan. 6, 1997–Present	
Richard Pombo (R-Calif.)	Jan. 5, 1993–Present	Resources Committee Chairman
David Price (D-N.C.)	Jan. 6, 1997–Present	Price also served from Jan. 3, 1987, to Jan. 3, 1995.
Deborah Pryce (R-Ohio)	Jan. 5, 1993–Present	
Charlie Rangel (D-N.Y.)	Jan. 21, 1971–Present	Ways and Means Committee, ranking member
Sam Rayburn (D-Tex.)	Mar. 4, 1913–Nov. 16, 1961	Former Speaker
Ralph Regula (R-Ohio)	Jan. 3, 1973–Present	
Thomas Reynolds (R-N.Y.)	Jan. 6, 1999–Present	National Republican Congressional Committee Chairman

House Member	Dates of Service	Leadership Post or Committee Chairmanship
Lynn Rivers (D-Mich.)	Jan. 3, 1995–Jan 3, 2003	
Hal Rogers (R-Ky.)	Jan. 5, 1981–Present	
Mike Rogers (R-Mich.)	Jan. 3, 2001–Present	
Dan Rostenkowski (D-Ill.)	Jan. 3, 1959–Jan. 3, 1995	Former Ways and Means Committee Chairman
Rick Santorum (R-Penn.)	Jan. 3, 1991–Jan. 3, 1995	
Charles Schumer (D-N.Y.)	Jan. 3, 1981–Jan. 3, 1999	
F. James Sensenbrenner (R-Wis.)	Jan. 25, 1979–Present	Judiciary Committee Chairman
Christopher Shays (R-Conn.)	Aug. 18, 1987–Present	
Brad Sherman (D-Calif.)	Jan. 6, 1997–Present	
Bud Shuster (R-Penn.)	Jan. 3, 1973–Feb. 3, 2001	Former Transportation and Infrastructure Committee Chairman
Rob Simmons (R-Conn.)	Jan. 3, 2001–Present	
Christopher Smith (R-N.J.)	Jan. 5, 1981–Present	Former Veterans Affairs Committee Chairman
Gerald B. H. Solomon (R-N.Y.)	Jan. 3, 1979–Jan. 3, 1999	Former Rules Committee Chairman
Mark Souder (R-Ind.)	Jan. 4, 1995–Present	
Fortney "Pete" Stark (D-Calif.)	Jan. 3, 1973–Present	
Charlie Stenholm (D-Tex.)	Jan. 3, 1979–Jan. 3, 2005	Former Agriculture Committee, ranking member
John Tanner (D-Tenn.)	Jan. 3, 1989–Present	
Ellen Tauscher (D-Calif.)	Jan. 6, 1997–Present	
W. J. "Billy" Tauzin (R-La.)	May 22, 1980–Jan. 3, 2005	Former Energy and Commerce Committee Chairman
Gene Taylor (D-Miss.)	Oct. 17, 1989–Present	
William M. Thomas (R-Calif.)	Jan. 15, 1979–Present	Ways and Means Committee Chairman
Mike Thompson (D-Calif.)	Jan. 6, 1999–Present	
Edolphus Towns (D-N.Y.)	Jan. 3, 1983–Present	
Fred Upton (R-Mich.)	Jan. 6, 1987–Present	
David Vitter (R-La.)	May 29, 1999–Jan. 3, 2005	
Robert Walker (R-Penn.)	Jan. 3, 1977–Jan. 3, 1997	Former Science Committee Chairman
Zach Wamp (R-Tenn.)	Jan. 4, 1995–Present	
Henry Waxman (D-Calif.)	Jan. 14, 1975–Present	
Vin Weber (R-Minn.)	Jan. 3, 1981–Jan. 3, 1993	
Heather Wilson (R-N.M.)	June 23, 1998–Present	
Joe Wilson (R-S.C.)	Dec. 18, 2001–Present	
Jim Wright (D-Tex.)	Jan. 3, 1955–June 30, 1989	Former Speaker
David Wu (D-Ore.)	Jan. 6, 1999–Present	
Don Young (R-Alaska)	Mar. 6, 1973–Present	Transportation and Infrastructure Committee Chairman

APPENDIX B

House Minority Leader Richard A. Gephardt's (D-Mo.) Remarks regarding the Impeachment of President Clinton

Washington, DC—House Minority Leader Richard A. Gephardt (D-Mo.) made the following statement on December 19, 1998:

Mr. Speaker, I stood on this floor yesterday and implored all of us to say that the politics of slash and burn must end. I implored all of us that we must turn away from the politics of personal destruction and return to the politics of values.

It is with that same passion that I say to all of you today that the gentleman from Louisiana (Mr. Bob Livingston) is a worthy and good and honorable man.

I believe his decision to retire is a terrible capitulation to the negative forces that are consuming our political system and our country, and I pray with all my heart that he will reconsider this decision.

Our Founding Fathers created a system of government of men, not of angels. No one standing in this House today can pass the puritanical test of purity that some are demanding that our elected leaders take. If we demand that mere mortals live up to this standard, we will see our seats of government lay empty and we will see the best, most able people unfairly cast out of public service.

We need to stop destroying imperfect people at the altar of an unobtainable morality. We need to start living up to the standards which the public in its infinite wisdom understands, that imperfect people must strive towards, but too often fall short.

We are now rapidly descending into a politics where life imitates farce, fratricide dominates our public debate, and America is held hostage to tactics of smear and fear.

Let all of us here today say no to resignation, no to impeachment, no to hatred, no to intolerance of each other, and no to vicious self-righteousness.

We need to start healing. We need to start binding up our wounds. We need to end this downward spiral which will culminate in the death of representative democracy.

I believe this healing can start today by changing the course we have begun. This is exactly why we need this today to be bipartisan. This is why we ask the opportunity to vote on a bipartisan censure resolution, to begin the process of healing our Nation and healing our people.

We are on the brink of the abyss. The only way we stop this insanity is through the force of our own will. The only way we stop this spiral is for all of us to finally say "enough." Let us step back from the abyss and let us begin a new politics of respect and fairness and decency, which realizes what has come before.

May God have mercy on this Congress, and may Congress have the wisdom and the courage and the goodness to save itself today.

Statement by House Speaker J. Dennis Hastert (R-Ill.) regarding the House Chaplain

Washington, DC—House Speaker J. Dennis Hastert (R-Ill.) made the following statement on March 23, 2000:

Mr. Speaker, I rise today on a point of personal privilege.

I come to this well today following a long period of prayerful consideration. I want to talk to you about the choice of our next Chaplain, a man whose job it is to ask God's blessing on our work.

When I became your Speaker last year, I stood in this very spot and said that this House needed to heal. Impeachment had hardened the hearts of too many of our members and ruptured the trust necessary for effective legislating.

Frankly, we had made progress toward that end. We successfully worked together to bring economic security to our country, to strengthen our schools and our national defense. And working together, we lowered our rhetoric from this well and returned some sense of civility to this chamber.

When I first heard that our current Chaplain wanted to retire, I decided I wanted to build on that growing sense of trust. Instead of simply appointing a Chaplain as some of my predecessors have done, I appointed the largest and most bipartisan search committee in the history of the House.

I want to take a moment to describe that process because it has been much distorted in the last four months.

I knew that finding the right person would be difficult. Many religious faiths are represented in this House, and many of you had candidates you believed would be good for the job. The Search Committee Dick Gephardt and I created was asked to review the many applicants and send to the leadership up to three, unranked candidates for final consideration.

I suppose that the Committee could have ignored those instructions and sent us only one candidate because they believed he or she was so far superior, that they stood out above all other applicants.

But they did not. In fact, I learned recently that the Search Committee discussed that very option and rejected it.

Instead, the committee, under the able leadership of Tom Bliley, a Catholic, and Earl Pomeroy, a Presbyterian, selected three outstanding candidates, Rev. Robert Dvorak, Father Tim O'Brien and Dr. Charles Wright.

These names were sent to us in alphabetical order. There was no ranking of the candidates. There was no "first choice" of the committee, as some would have the public believe. In fact, there could *not* be a "first choice" because the committee never set out to select one. The report to this House by the bipartisan co-chairmen of the committee makes this fact abundantly clear. The truth is simple: each of the three candidates was deemed as acceptable to the Search Committee.

Along with Majority Leader Armey and Minority Leader Gephardt, I interviewed the three candidates sent to us by the bipartisan Search Committee.

I was looking for a kind person, with a caring heart. I was looking for a person who had extensive counseling and pastoral or parish experience. I was looking for a person who Members of Congress could take their problems to and find reassurance and wisdom.

I was not looking for a particular denomination or faith, and I didn't make my selection based on the candidate's religious doctrine or the past history of House Chaplains. I was trying to be fair to all candidates.

While I found all three candidates to have impressive credentials, I was most impressed with the pastoral experience and warmth of Dr. Charles Wright, who for years has ministered to the needs of the Capitol Hill community. In addition he had years of experience in the inner city as well as the international community. He spent years trying to break down the walls of apartheid and seek common understanding between blacks and whites. I made my selection based on that experience and on the qualities I found in him. No one, other than the candidates themselves, influenced my decision. Any suggestion to the contrary is simply wrong.

After the interviews and a period of reflection, I consulted with the Majority Leader and the Minority Leader twice before I made my final decision. In the first discussion one preferred Dr. Wright and one preferred Rev. Dvorak. In the second discussion, one preferred Dr. Wright and one preferred Father O'Brien. The choice was not unanimous but both signed off on the choice of Dr. Wright and we issued a joint press release announcing the selection. I thought we had reached consensus.

Following our joint press statement there were immediate charges of anti-Catholic bigotry. I was surprised and disappointed. Since there was no bias in the decision, I assumed that the disappointment held by some that a Catholic was not chosen would go away when people understood the truth. I was wrong.

I then thought that once the Search Committee issued their report and laid out the facts of the selection process that the controversy would be over. Sadly, the facts were ignored and the controversy continued to be stoked. It was then that I realized that a far more serious effort was afoot—some were trying to take political advantage out of what was essentially a spiritual decision and charged me with anti-Catholic sentiment.

Is there anti-Catholic sentiment still alive in our country? In fact, is there anti-religious bias alive in our country?

Sad as it is to admit I believe the answer to both these questions may be yes. This bias comes in many shapes and sizes, whether it be the television shows that hold the Church in contempt, the activists who desecrate St. Patrick's Cathedral, or the so called "artists" who denigrate important religious symbols. My friends, that is anti-Catholic and anti-religious bias.

Certainly, there are those who differ with some of the view held by the Catholic Church. Even some Catholics respectfully disagree with some Church positions. I agree with the Catholic Church on many things.

I agree with the Catholic Church that we should protect the unborn. I agree with the mission of the Catholic schools, who help so many Catholic and non-Catholic students get a values-based education. I wholeheartedly support the Catholic Church's great work to help the poor.

I believe that the Vatican should have a seat in the United Nations. And I have the greatest respect and admiration for the Pope, who has done so much to bring peace to our troubled world and played such a critical role in ending the scourge of Communism in Eastern Europe.

I am a patient man. In my role as Speaker of the whole House, I believe I should try to be especially patient, and seek compromise and not confrontation. But even I do not easily take in stride carelessly tossed accusations of bigotry. Where I come from, such slander is an ugly business. I can only conclude that those who accuse me of anti-Catholic bigotry either don't know me or are maliciously seeking political advantage by making these accusations.

The institution of this House means a great deal to me. I believe each of us, as Members of this House, should look out for this institution and treat it with respect. As your Speaker, I feel a special burden to do so. And it is with that conviction that I say to each of you that I believe the political maneuvering on this issue may have catastrophic unintended consequences—like children playing with matches.

In fact, in light of this controversy, some critics now advocate that we get rid of the Office of the Chaplain altogether. There are editorials being written to that effect in papers around this country. I ask each of you to search your heart: Is that what is good for this institution? I hope your answer is no. But that, my friends, is where these political games could be taking us.

I think to lose the Office of the Chaplain would be a grave mistake.

Ever since the first prayer was offered in the Continental Congress on September 7, 1774, two years before the Declaration of Independence was written, Congress has been blessed by a daily prayer. The daily prayer has served as a peaceful refuge from the partisan wrangling. It has bound disparate factions under the unifying theme of God's love.

The First Amendment to the Constitution states clearly that "Congress should make no law respecting an establishment of religion." But at the same time the rules and precedents of this House say that "the chaplain shall attend at the commencement of the House and open the same with prayer."

These contrary impulses signify two great American themes: Americans should have the freedom to practice any religion they want, but Americans also believe that this nation was founded under God to fulfill a greater mission.

The House Chaplain must reflect both traditions. The chaplain of the House must submerge his or her own doctrinal views while reaching out to all members, regardless of religious faith. He must say a prayer that unites us rather than divides us.

Our current House Chaplain, Jim Ford, has blessed us with daily prayers and counseled Members quietly, with honesty and integrity. Jim Ford is a Lutheran, but he has not preached Lutheran doctrine from the House pulpit. His message is universal.

In fact, Tip O'Neill, an Irish Catholic, and our respected former

Speaker, often called Jim Ford "Monsignor," as a way to signify his approval of Ford's universal message.

I believe that any representative of any religion can provide a similar universal message for the House of Representatives.

My support for Charles Wright had nothing to do with Dr. Wright's denomination nor his religious doctrine. Of the three candidates presented to me by the Committee, I believed he had the best ability to help members of the House, based on his extensive experience in counseling. I agree with our colleague Tony Hall, who first suggested to Dr. Wright that he apply, that first and foremost Charles Wright has a pastor's heart.

Sadly, it has become clear to me that the minority will never support Charles Wright to be the House Chaplain. I have waited more than four months in the hope that voices of reason would prevail.

Charles Wright is a good and decent man. He would make an excellent Chaplain. That is why I asked Leader Gephardt to allow him to meet with the Democratic Caucus. That is why our colleague, Tony Hall, a man whose respect in this House is unmatched, made the same request. But these requests have not been fulfilled.

Instead of hearing the positive voice of a Godly and caring man, the only voices we hear are whispered hints in dark places that his selection is the result of anti-Catholic bias.

My friends, in all of my years in this Congress, I have never seen a more cynical and more destructive political campaign. That such a campaign should be waged in connection with the selection of the House Chaplain brings shame on this House.

During the interview process, Dick Gephardt explained very eloquently to one of the candidates that democracy was a substitute for war. He was warning the candidate that if he became the Chaplain his flock would not always behave like folks on a Sunday picnic. He went on to say that unlike war, where men set out to destroy one another, in a democracy we were constrained by a set of rules and a common decency. It was a moving and profound observation that I have thought a lot about.

But I must say that the history of this Chaplain issue over the last four months does not appear to be constrained by common decency. It looks a lot like war. And it has an ugly face. This institution, so important in the protection of our freedom, is more important than which one of us sits in that Speaker's chair.

In the light of this controversy, Charles Wright has told me that he does not want to serve as Chaplain in a divided House. I reluctantly agreed that I would accept his decision not to be our Chaplain. I regret that decision of Dr. Wright, but I understand it.

So, where do we go from here?

As the Speaker of this Whole House, I will act to stop those who want to persist in this unseemly political game. I will not allow this House to be torn apart and the Office of the Chaplain to be destroyed.

Having formally received the resignation of Chaplain Ford, I am today, under the authority granted to me under the rules and precedents of this House to fill vacancies, naming Daniel Coughlin *(Cog-lin)* to serve as Chaplain of the House.

Father Coughlin is the vicar of the Archdiocese of Chicago and comes with the highest recommendations from a man of God for whom I have great respect, my good friend Cardinal George of Chicago.

I believe that Daniel Coughlin will bring to the House a caring and healing heart. He has been a parish priest and has spent the past several years counseling parish priests within the Archdiocese. He brings 40 years of ministerial experience to this House.

Daniel Coughlin is a Catholic. That does not make him more nor less qualified for the job. But I am proud of his historic appointment. And I hope his appointment will help us to heal—and that it will bring a sense of pride to the millions of Catholic men and women around this country who have had legitimate feelings of past discrimination which some in this House have sought to manipulate.

I urge all of my colleagues to get to know Father Coughlin. He is a good man who will provide this House with the spiritual guidance and counseling support necessary to bring us together again.

Let me say to every leader of this House and to every member of this House, let us embrace our new Chaplain, put this episode behind us, and move forward to do the people's business.

Address by House Speaker J. Dennis Hastert "Reflections on the Role of the Speaker in the Modern Day House of Representatives"

On November 12, 2003, House Speaker J. Dennis Hastert delivered the following address at the Library of Congress.

Bob [referring to former House Republican Leader Robert H. Michel], thank you for that kind introduction. I want to thank you, Bob, for what you have meant to me. You were my first mentor here in Washington. You, Bob, the man who should have and deserved to be Speaker, taught me the value of patience. You took me under your wing when I first came to Congress, and showed me how Congress worked. You helped me with my Committee assignments, and gave me my first leadership responsibility . . . heading up the Republican Leaders Health Care Task Force in response to First Lady Hillary Clinton's efforts on health care. You taught me that it is the workhorse who wins in the legislative game, not the show horse. Your cheerful demeanor hid a will of steel, and your abundant common-sense served your colleagues and your country well. Bob, we know that you are going through a tough time with loss of your beloved wife Corinne. We share your grief. Know that our thoughts and prayers are with you during this most difficult time.

I appreciate this opportunity to reflect on my current job. Clearly, the role of Speaker has changed over the years. It has changed because of the times, because of those who have occupied the office, and because of the nature of the institution. Joseph Cannon, the man from Danville, ruled from the Speaker's Chair with Iron power. Tip O'Neill ruled with Irish charm. Newt Gingrich brought star power to the office. Sam Rayburn ruled for a generation, while Joe Martin had only a fleeting chance to assert Republican control. Each used their principles to guide them in times of great challenge.

O'Neill was challenged by a popular President, Carl Albert was challenged by a Constitutional crisis, Rayburn through war, and Tom Foley by a series of institutional crises. I have my own set of principles that have worked for me.

I never thought I would be Speaker. I didn't run for the job. I didn't campaign for it. I didn't play the P.R. game. I just did my job as best I could for my constituents and for my colleagues. In fact, if you had asked me to predict Newt Gingrich's successor, I wouldn't have been on my own list.

My first principle is one I learned from my friend Bob Michel. To be good at the job of Speaker, you must be willing to put in the time to be a good listener. By this, I mean you must listen to the members of the House. Before I became Speaker, I thought I knew the importance of paying attention to member's needs. I had served in the Whip organization when Bob Michel was leader and I served as Chief Deputy Whip when Newt became Speaker. When you are a Whip, you need to listen, because to get and win votes, you need to hear what the members are saying. But when you are Speaker, the sheer volume of voices is increased, and the problems become more difficult to solve. I learned that the best way to find solutions was to get people around the table to talk it through. When you have a small majority, like I have had for pretty much my entire tenure, you have to do a lot of listening. And when you talk, you have to keep your word.

That brings me to my second principle. When you are Speaker, people expect you to keep your word, and they will not quickly forgive you if you cannot deliver. I learned that keeping your word is the most important part of this job. You are better off not saying anything than making a promise that you cannot keep. And you have to keep both the big promises and the small promises.

My third principle is that a Speaker must respect the power of regular order. I am a regular order guy. I think it is important to rely on the Committees to do their hearings and mark-ups. I don't like to create task forces to craft legislation. The Committees are there for a reason, and we should use them. There are times when you need to establish working groups to coordinate the work of standing committees when big projects cross jurisdictional lines, but those working groups should "coordinate" not supplant the Committee structure. I have also found that it is easy to find the problems in legislation through the Committee process.

My fourth principle is that while a Speaker should strive to be fair, he also is judged by how he gets the job done. The job of the Speaker is to rule fairly, but ultimately to carry out the will of the Majority. Unlike some other parliamentary bodies, the Speaker in the U.S. House is the leader of his party. He is not merely a disinterested arbiter of parliamentary rules. This creates a unique tension within the office of the Speaker. It is not always easy to be fair when you have a vested interest in the outcome. But if the Chair is seen as being unfair, the likely result is a breakdown in parliamentary comity. We take the job of fairness very seriously. We seek out our best parliamentary experts to serve in the Chair as Speakers Pro Tem, people like Ray LaHood, Doc Hastings, Mac Thornberry, Mike Simpson and others. We also have professional Parliamentarians who are avowedly non-partisan. Charlie and his team play a critical role in advising me on jurisdictional referrals and parliamentary judgments from the Chair. This is tradition stretching back beyond Louis Deschler, and it is a good tradition. We make certain that those serving in the Chair do not serve on the Committees of Jurisdiction for the business on the floor. And we try to be fair in the Rules Committee process. We guarantee the Minority the right to recommit the bill with instructions, giving them one last chance to make their best arguments to amend the pending legislation. But while we strive to be fair, we also strive to get the job done. We are not the Senate. The rules of the House, while they protect the rights of the Minority, they also insure that the will of the majority of the House will prevail. So, on occasion, you will see us take effective action to get the job done. Sometimes, we have a hard time convincing the majority of the House to vote like a majority of the House, so sometimes you will see votes stay open longer than usual. But the hallmark of an effective leadership is one that can deliver the votes. And we have been an effective leadership.

My fifth principle is to please the majority of the majority. On occasion, a particular issue might excite a majority made up mostly of the minority. Campaign finance is a particularly good example of this phenomenon. The job of Speaker is not to expedite legislation that runs counter to the wishes of the majority of his majority. As in campaign finance reform, our majority thought it was a bad bill that weakened the party structure and promoted abuse by special interests. As a side note, the emergence of 527 organizations in the next election will prove our point that special interests, and not political parties, will have more influence because of campaign finance reform. So we fought the efforts by advocates of campaign regulation to pass it. They did what they thought they had to do, getting enough signatures to sign a discharge petition. I made them go through that process twice in order to prove two points. First, I wanted my troops to know I opposed the bill. Second, I wanted to let them know that I had no choice but to schedule the legislation. I was not going to abandon my party's position under any circumstances. On each piece of legislation, I actively seek to bring our party together. I do not feel comfortable scheduling any controversial legislation unless I know we have the votes on our side first.

My sixth principle is the Speaker's job is to focus on the House and nothing but the House. This is a big job. It is a time consuming job. And it is an exhausting job. I said that when I became Speaker, I would focus only on running the House. And I found out that means more than just sitting in the Speaker's chair. It means doing those things necessary to keeping the majority, whether that means fund-raising for incumbents or campaigning for challengers. You don't see me spending too much time on television shows, or giving big speeches. I have no interest in running for President or making the jump to the Senate. This is an important and big job. And it requires singular focus to get it done.

My final principle is my most important principle: Never forget who sent you to Congress in the first place: your constituents. I get home to Illinois every weekend. Of course, it is nice to see my wife, who inevitably gives me a list of chores to complete when I get there. But it is also important to see my friends and my constituents. It is very easy to get lost in the muddle of Washington D.C. The world of amendments, campaign fundraisers, motions to recommit, and jurisdictional battles, all of which are foreign to Yorkville, Illinois. As a matter of fact, most of my constituents are none too impressed with the trappings of power. My constituents sent me to Washington not to argue, not to debate. They sent me here to get the job done. They are not content to play the blame game, they don't want to hear about how this bill died in the House or that bill died in the Senate. They want us to pass laws that make their lives better. When I go home, I am not Mr. Speaker. To my wife and friends and voters, I am Denny. And I tell you, that healthy dose of humility does me a world of good every time I come back here to Washington. It helps me to connect to what the American people are really thinking about, and it helps me to understand what concerns my colleagues are facing.

At the end of the day, the Speaker of the House is really just the guy who stands up for the people of America. In our Constitution, the Speaker of the House is the first officer mentioned, because in our system of government, it is the people who rule. Since January of 1999, I have had the great honor and privilege to be that guy.

Thank you for inviting me here today for this most fascinating symposium.

I wish you the best of luck for the rest of the day.

INDEX